Taking Care

Lessons from Mothers with Disabilities

Mary Grimley Mason
with Linda Long-Bellil

University Press of America,® Inc.
Lanham • Boulder • New York • Toronto • Plymouth, UK

Copyright © 2012 by University Press of America,® Inc.
4501 Forbes Boulevard, Suite 200, Lanham, Maryland 20706
UPA Aquisitions Department (301) 459-3366

10 Thornbury Road, Plymouth PL6 7PP, United Kingdom

British Library Cataloguing in Publication Information Available

Library of Congress Control Number: 2012943502
ISBN: 978-0-7618-5969-7 (paper : alk. paper)—ISBN: 978-0-7618-5970-3 (electronic)

Cover photograph by Anthony Fernandez

To all of the mothers who so generously shared their stories

Contents

Acknowledgments

When I approached my colleague, Linda Long-Bellil, about joining me in this project on mothers with disabilities, neither of us knew how long the journey would be to its completion. Delays of one sort and another kept coming up, but we are glad we persevered. Linda has done some of the interviews and her excellent essay on public policy and mothers with disabilities brings the stories of these women's experiences to a close.

My friend Gail Pool, writer, editor, and reviewer, encouraged me to believe in my approach to this subject. She also read some of the early chapters, providing practical and wise advice. Carol Hurd Green, whose valued long friendship includes our collaboration on two edited books, brought her fine editorial skills to the final version of the manuscript. Marie Gurry, my colleague from Emmanuel College, did careful formatting for me.

The community of women scholars at Brandeis University's Women's Studies Research Center (WSRC) has provided a stimulating and caring environment for my work. Shulamit Rhineharz, the director, has given me support and encouragement for my research and activism in Disability Studies. A grant from the Tarvis Fund helped with research expenses. My memoir writing group, with whom I have worked for many years, read some of the early material and gave thoughtful responses. Karin Frostig, a member of that group, was particularly insightful when we shared each other's work. I have had some wonderful student assistants in the WSRC Scholar-Partners Program, including Avi Goldman and Sarah Linet, whose moving essay on growing up with a disabled mother is in the last chapter.

A version of the story of Phouvieng in chapter I was published in The WIP (Women's International Perspective), "Transcending Stereotypes: Parenting with a Disability," March 11, 2009. Material in the Introduction about my children was based on my essay that became a performance piece created by Nurit Eine-Pindyck. With the help of a grant from the Shelley Tyre Fund, the piece was edited for YouTube as "Taking Care: A Disabled Mother's Dialogue with her Daughter."

Finally, I'd like to thank my children, Cathleen, Paul and Sarah, who have always been supportive of my work and who encourage me with their love and care.

Introduction

Disability and the Role of Mothering

"This is the hardest thing you will ever do," says Melanie, a young disabled mother with cerebral palsy, about raising a child, but she goes on to say that it is fulfilling, joyous and "an amazing gift." Melanie's voice echoes many mothers with disabilities, who share many issues about parenting with all mothers but who have additional social, environmental and physical barriers to overcome in caring for their children.

"Taking Care: Lessons from Mothers with Disabilities" gathers together some of the lessons learned from the experiences of disabled mothers. The successes of these women as mothers challenge stereotypes about good mothering: the barriers they encounter show the need for better accommodations from the society in which they live. The book, based on twenty-six interviews and other autobiographical narratives, covers the mothering cycle from pregnancy and birth to raising a child through young adulthood. Despite the special challenges disabled parents face, approximately 8 million adults with disabilities in the United States are parents. The higher percentage are disabled women.

When I joined the feminist movement in the seventies, I became aware that I belonged to another community of women—women with disabilities. Though I had polio as a child, I had not previously identified with the disability community. My new interest led me to writing a book, *Working Against Odds: Stories of Disabled Women's Work Lives*. Ten of the women in that book were mothers and when I heard their stories, I knew I wanted to know more about the lives of other disabled mothers.

As a mother of three adult children and four grandchildren, I can look back and see some of the issues I faced. When I wrote my memoir, *Life*

Prints: A Memoir of Healing and Discovery, I asked my children how they felt about growing up with a disabled mother. They did not come up with many answers. Later, Sally, my youngest child, wrote on her website about her reactions to living in a family with a disabled parent. She described struggling, as a child, between guilt at being able-bodied with a disabled mother "so brave" and resentment at having to take care of someone else's needs. Her essay began a dialogue between us, which came to include my other two children.

I realized that growing up with a disabled mother had probably influenced their lives significantly and it was clear that each child's experience differed depending on age and place in the family. All three of them, however, have chosen careers or avocations that focus on helping others. My eldest daughter, Kathryn, is comfortable in the role of the caring older sister. Her father left the family and we divorced as she was finishing college. She went on to do graduate work in clinical psychology and has become a therapist. Matt, the middle child and only son, felt the need to prove his self-sufficiency after his father left. He worked through college and law school and went on to practice law. His first job was in legal aid. Sally, the youngest, experienced abandonment when she was left at home without her father or her siblings. After college and several different jobs, she moved to California to pursue writing and the arts. She also started the first web site for women with eating disorders and became an activist in Washington for better funding for mental health.

Our family's conversations also made me realize that I often overcompensated and tried to become a super mom. The dialogue with my younger daughter helped me to recognize that we had both felt guilty and had been unable to reach out to each other during the particularly difficult years in our family. I came away from these discussions feeling I was not a super mom but that I had done a pretty good job of mothering. I could not always perform all of the tasks of mothering, but my children were satisfied with my role as a mother. My reflections about my children and our conversations motivated me to find out what other disabled mothers felt about mothering. What does "taking care" of their children mean to them? And how do they do it? These questions and many more became part of the inquiry I wanted to pursue.

As I interviewed these women included here, I realized that although every person's story is unique, we shared some common themes about self-identity as mothers and about our roles as mothers. Like all persons with disabilities, we experience the discrimination of institutionalized ableism, the cultural construct that dictates that ablebodiness is the "norm." (Campbell, 2008) Rosemarie Garland Thomson (1997), discussing this normative concept, coined the term "normate," to represent the social figure that feels uniquely qualified to be "normal" and thus a definitive human being (p. 8).

All of us who fall outside of this norm of ablebodiness become "the Other." The acceptance of a definitive norm is embedded in all of our institutions including the educational and medical establishments and the cultural and social institutions. As persons with disabilities, we are singled out as not belonging, thus making it easier for others to feel they do belong (Davis, 2000, pp.104-105).

As mothers with disabilities we are particularly vulnerable to this social exclusion. First, as disabled women we often feel seen as imperfect women—as asexual, dependent and unable to fulfill traditional female roles. Then as mothers we confront society's ideal of the "good mother," who is perfect and "a natural caregiver," an unattainable norm for any woman, but particularly a woman with a disability. Although feminists from Adrienne Rich to postmodernists have tried to counteract these cultural misrepresentations, they still exist. As a mother, the disabled woman often internalizes negative perceptions of herself as a woman and in addition, strives to achieve the impossible cultural expectations of motherhood. She struggles to prove that she is at least a "good enough" mother.

I found, in addition, that mothers with disabilities share the unusual position of being both a caregiver and a care receiver, while being perceived primarily as a care receiver. This duality is often a source of anxiety. The amount of care a disabled mother needs can vary a great deal, from the need for personal assistance with activities of daily living to minor assistance with heavy chores or perhaps intermittent attention to issues of chronic illness. The position is still the same. A disabled mother is placed in the middle of competing priorities—attending to her own needs and fulfilling her role of taking care of her child. The primary domain of mothering has always been defined as care giving, particularly physical care. Even scholars such as Sara Ruddick (1995), who in *Maternal Thinking* argues against the idea of the "natural mother," still defines the role of mothering as protective, nurturing and caring. This characterization makes us, as disabled mothers, who have physical limitations and may need some care ourselves, feel anxious about our role as a mother.

Another commonality shared by mothers with disabilities is in their relationship with the professional world of care giving. Health professionals and social service providers often reinforce the anxiety in disabled mothers about their dual role. The providers are frequently ill informed about the capabilities of disabled mothers and they are used to thinking of these women as passive receivers of care. They distrust disabled women's competence in raising a child and they often overlook the ingenious ways such mothers adapt and perform even the most physical tasks such as carrying, feeding, dressing and bathing their infants or young children.

Social service providers sometimes go a step further in their mistrust of disabled mothers. They intervene unnecessarily, even removing a child from the home over concerns about safety or about children being asked to help disabled parents too much. Children who carry out specific tasks for a parent are identified as victims of "parenting the parent," an attitude particularly prevalent in Britain in the 1990s (Olsen and Clarke, 2003). Fortunately, this attitude has been changing. More recently, (Mullin, 2005) studies show that except in obvious cases of oppressive or burdensome care giving, children can gain from helping and should have the opportunity to recognize others' needs. Nevertheless, when compounded by prejudicial factors such as being a single parent or economically disadvantaged, disabled mothers often experience the fear that they will be judged as unfit and that their children will be taken away.

The medical establishment sometimes is also skeptical about a disabled woman becoming a successful mother. Too often doctors see a disabled woman as someone who is sick and needs to be cured, not as someone who aspires to live an ordinary life that includes having children. Disabled women find that doctors know very little about their reproductive health. In fact, according to a report in 1992 from the Connecticut Department of Public Health, many women with disabilities have been actually physically injured during gynecological examinations or procedures due to the medical personnel's lack of experience and knowledge (Richman, 2005). Because of their lack of knowledge about disabilities and their habit of being in control of a woman's reproductive health, doctors sometime discourage disabled women from becoming mothers, fearing unknown complications in pregnancy and childbirth. Some fear the risk of the women producing "defective" babies even if the disability is only rarely genetically carried.

Perhaps there is still a residual attitude in the medical world that pregnancy is a condition to be treated and not a natural part of a women's reproductive cycle. Perhaps we still suffer from echoes of the 19th century when eminent doctors such as E. H. Dixon wrote books specifically for women entitled *Women and her Diseases from Cradle to the Grave*. Pregnancy was treated like a disease because it subjected a woman to "a great variety of ailments" (Herndl, 2002, p.265). With this patriarchal heritage in the medical world, it is no wonder that women with disabilities, already seen as medically unfit, are often advised by doctors not to become mothers or if pregnant, counseled to have an abortion.

There are some positive signs that the medical world is becoming aware of the special needs of women with disabilities. One report argues that medical professionals have developed innovative approaches and awareness to help disabled women through pregnancy and delivery (Madorsky, 1995, p. 153). Other reports are not so optimistic and argue that society's negative views and attitudes about disability, particularly about disabled women as mothers, reinforce the medical world's prejudices and stifle creative thinking. They argue that we need to change society's attitude toward all people with disabilities.

Disability advocates for mothers with disabilities agree that social attitudes as well as health care practices must change. New ways of thinking could provide disabled mothers with more assistance with caring for their children. Although disabled mothers may count on informal assistance from family, spouse, and friends they may also need formal, funded assistance from healthcare providers. The latter, referred to by one scholar as a "ramp to motherhood" (Prilleltensky, 2003, p. 37) is often hard to come by. Services available are inconsistent and vary regionally. A disabled mother who gets personal care assistance for herself (help with daily activities of living such as dressing, bathing etc.) cannot, in most states, use that assistance to help her with tasks for caring for her child. On the other hand, sometimes a disabled mother, who does not need a personal care assistant, can be told that she is not "sick enough" to qualify for homecare that would make her life easier as a mother. Studies have shown that given even a small amount of help in performing difficult physical tasks, a disabled mother can feel independent, particularly if the assistant, allowing the mother to be the primary carer, stays in the background until needed. This "nurturing assistant," as it has been called, is part of the reevaluation of care giving advocated by feminists, such as Susan Wendell (1997) and Barbara Hillyer (1993), who advocate women-centered practices of care that emphasize the importance of reciprocity in the care giving relationship.

Considering that a disabled mother may be viewed as an imperfect woman, a possible biological risk as a reproducer, a dependent person who is a care receiver, and a mother who cannot protect her child, it is no wonder that a mother with a disability can feel "under a societal magnifying glass" (Prilleltensky, 2003, p. 23). In the public sphere of schools and communities and commerce and in the private sphere of family, friends, even neighbors and strangers, she needs to constantly prove her competency as a mother.

Many of the younger women I interviewed, who have grown up with the disability movement or at least become mothers since the movement's impact, do not accept these stereotypes. They know they cannot do everything some mothers can, but they know that with the proper resources, they can be a good mother. Many fight for better resources—greater access, better childcare and assistance—and more understanding of their needs. They go to school meetings and attend their children's classes and try to enlighten others about what they CAN do, as disabled mothers. They have taken advantage of online sites, such as DAWN (Disabled Women's Network Ontario) and "Parents with Disabilities Online," which offer helpful advice. Among organizations, "Through The Looking Glass," which is a national center that was one of the first to pursue research about parents with disabilities, offers training and services to disabled parents and families. Some disabled mothers have developed blogs themselves and others have found support in organizations for their particular disability, such as the National Spinal Cord Injury Association.

However, all of the women interviewed and others who share writings have experienced some discrimination. For instance, several were discouraged from having a child as if the whole idea of their being a mother was irrational. One woman with cerebral palsy wrote about being thrilled to discover that she was pregnant only to have her doctor suggest that she think seriously about an abortion. Another woman, who was pregnant when she had a spinal cord injury in a car accident, said the doctors just assumed that she would put her child up for adoption.

One of the "lessons" many of the mothers conveyed in these interviews was the importance of finding a knowledgeable and sympathetic doctor and closely monitoring their care. At least one woman changed her obstetrician when she found that the doctor did not know anything about how her disability might affect her pregnancy and delivery. In fact, it was unusual, it seems, to find doctors who were well informed about the effects of specific disabilities.

Other women interviewed had unfortunate experiences from health care providers and social services. Several found nurses and social workers ill informed and unhelpful. One young woman with cerebral palsy had a particularly bad experience. Feeling overwhelmed with her young infant, she called a social service agency for assistance. They sent a woman who told the young mother that she was depressed and should leave her marriage. Another mother, a polio survivor and a single parent managing a two year old when she was pregnant with her second child, called social service agencies for some help and was told that they could only deal with people who weren't able to care for themselves.

Many women experienced the negative judgment of the outside world. Several mothers remembered feeling the disapproval of other women, even neighbors. One mother in a wheelchair said that neighbors called DSS (Department of Social Services) twice to complain that she was not properly supervising a swimming pool. In both occasions the DSS came and approved the pool. Several women had family members who were unsupportive. A young mother remembered that when she told her father that she was having a second child, he said, "You've already tempted fate once. Why do you want to do it again?"

My sources for these interviews with mothers with disabilities were from referrals, newsletters of organizations of particular disabilities, such as the National Spinal Cord Injury Association, and from Independent Living Centers. From the many responses and offers to volunteer for an interview, I chose a group of twenty-five women (the twenty sixth interview was with a young able-bodied woman). They represent a wide geographical sampling—

Arkansas, California, Georgia, Kansas, Massachusetts, New York, North Carolina and Ohio.

The women have diverse backgrounds in race, ethnicity, and class and their ages range from 30 to 75. Their personal lives are varied. Seventeen women were in a continuous marital relationship. Eight women had divorced and three had remarried. Seven women were primarily single mothers. Six women were married to men with a disability. The children's ages cover a wide range from one year old twins to preteens, teenagers, young adults and even two middle aged sons of 52 and 53.

The women's disabilities are limited to physical and sensory impairments although one woman has begun to experience cognitive impairments as well. Their physical disabilities are diverse, including cerebral palsy, spinal bifida, polio, spinal or brain injuries, multiple sclerosis, juvenile rheumatoid arthritis, dwarfism and hereditary spastic paraplegia. Two women were legally blind.

These stories of mothering are compelling because of the unique voices of the women which are apparent in their stories and their own words. Although they share common experiences as discussed above, their disabilities do not limit their individuality as women or mothers.

I have organized this book around the mothering cycle. The chapters are based on the women's experiences. They reflect the shared reality of being a mother with a disability. This includes their identity as a disabled mother, the double consciousness of being both a care giver and care receiver, the negotiations with the "norms" of the outside world, and finally, the tensions but also the mutual support of their children as they grow up. The major connecting theme or lesson that runs through all four chapters is the understanding that mothering, especially for a woman with a disability, involves interdependence with family, friends, or other forms of support. Each chapter focuses on the stories of four or five women who have been chosen to represent that particular phase of the motherhood cycle. The women have often agreed to be interviewed so that their experiences can be useful to other mothers with disabilities. Their experiences are often relevant to all mothers.

Chapter One, "Having a Child: From the Decision Through the Postpartum Experience," shows that for many of these women choosing to have a child defines the way they think about themselves as disabled women. It focuses primarily on the women's reproductive choices and the experience of birth, delivery and post partum care and early care giving. Chapter Two, "Care Giving and Women with Disabilities: The Early Years," focuses primarily on raising young children from infancy to pre-school. It explores the challenges of giving and receiving care, how these competing priorities can be negotiated and how these mothers adapt to the physical challenges they face in taking care of their children. Chapter Three, "Meeting the Outside World," is about helping children understand society's attitude to people with disabilities and teaching them about society's view of "the norm." It describes how the women often became advocates for people with disabilities. Finally, Chapter Four, " Family Relationships and Community," is about sharing needs and responsibilities with their children and about creating community that welcomes diversity.

Despite the discrimination, the challenges and the marginalization, the women I interviewed and read about have embraced motherhood enthusiastically. They find being a mother rewarding and self-empowering, but all of them said it was not easy. "I think it's hard for any mom and I think it's harder—no, I know it's harder for moms with disabilities," says one woman with cerebral palsy. When asked if they would advise other women with disabilities to have children, they all agreed that they would but cautioned that the women should speak to as many other disabled mothers as they could about "tips and tools" on how to do things and to have a plan. "Do your research," said one woman, and added, "The more you can go into it with open eyes, the fewer epiphanies you need to have after the fact." These women insisted that disabled women should not be discouraged from deciding to have children.

Many of the women emphasized that although they might not be able to perform all the tasks of care giving—many of them did with creative adaptability—they felt confident in their role of mothering and in nurturing their children. They defined their role as being available emotionally and psychologically. Even if they could not always participate physically, they could encourage their children's activities and aspirations. Many of the women felt that their children were better people for having to learn about some one else's needs and about diversity and community. One woman summed up the general attitude and shared conviction: "There's nothing we can't overcome, there's nothing we can't do together."

These women's stories reveal major themes which have shaped their experience of motherhood and which can offer a significant model for all parenting. Self-determination, interconnectedness and interdependence leading towards community are lessons they learn from all stages of their experience as mothers.

Chapter One

Having a Child

From the Decision through the Postpartum Experience

It is hard to imagine any young girl growing up in our society not having ideas about being a mother—probably looking forward to being one herself; or even feeling, for one reason or another, that she didn't have a great desire to be a mother.

Most young girls expect to be mothers and some see their coming of age as motherhood—whether wisely or not. Tradition, popular culture, and a thriving industry supplying goods for infants and children create powerful expectations and images of motherhood for young women, not always tested by reality.

Society does not expect women with disabilities to become mothers. As we'll see from the following stories, society often sees them as imperfect women, unable to fulfill the traditional female role of bearing and raising a child. However, these women interviewed were eager to have children. As a young girl, Cindy, who acquired a spinal cord injury at eighteen, had always imagined herself becoming a mother so the first thing she asked her doctor after her accident was "Can I still be a mom?" When he said yes, she says that she felt that her life was "still worth living."

Other women, with disabilities from birth or early in their life, spoke about how they expected to become a mother despite their disabilities. Donna, who had polio, says, "I always wanted to be a mom and it wasn't anything that I thought I couldn't do because I had a disability." Kathy, who has severe rheumatoid arthritis, says that her mother always assumed that Kathy would have a child and conveyed that expectation to her. However, not all of the women grew up with expectations of motherhood. Talia's family discouraged her from thinking that she could be a mother and she internalized that attitude so that when she was unexpectedly pregnant, she was at first, very fearful. Lorrie, born with cerebral palsy, remembers that although she "truly enjoyed kids" and even taught Sunday school, she didn't think she wanted to have children. Now, she can't imagine life without her two daughters.

Many of the women found motherhood transformative. And Debbie (2002), who is blind, writes of the transformative power of becoming a mother: "I reveled in the sense that I was joining a new community of motherhood. My blindness receded into the background. I was no longer an outsider. I was one of the initiated at last." (p. 63)

Before making a decision to take on the responsibility of being a mother, many of the women I interviewed asked themselves some hard questions:

"Will my child inherit my disability genetically and does it matter? Can I manage a pregnancy and safe delivery of a child? Can I take care of the child despite my disability?"

By asking these questions and wrestling with their decisions, the women often arrived at a better understanding of themselves as disabled women. They understood their capabilities better and their right to be validated as mothers.

They also recognized that for a woman with a disability, mothering involves collaborating with other people and balancing their determination to be independent with the need to accept some dependence. This is a major theme throughout this book.

1. THE GENETIC QUESTION: WILL MY CHILD INHERIT MY DISABILITY GENETICALLY AND DOES IT MATTER?

Molly: Everyone said it was okay. But it was totally not okay.

Molly, born in 1968 with HSP (Heredity Spastic Paraplegia), couldn't have predicted the change in attitude that occurred in her husband and his family when their son was diagnosed with the same neurological disability when he was five years old. She says, "Everyone knew that if we had a child, there was a possibility that the child would have HSP and his whole family embraced it." But when Rick, their son, was diagnosed with the disability, the whole family fell apart. "It was awful," she says, "Everyone said it was okay. But it totally was not okay. Which was a shocker to me."

Molly's HSP, which results in some instability in balance and walking (it affects about 25,000 people in the U.S.) is part of her family. Her grandfather and father had it. The chances, therefore, of passing on the gene to her child were quite good. Her family had no problem with that and Molly thought when she married and she and her husband decided to have children that he was also undisturbed by that. She discovered that was not exactly the case.

Molly says that growing up her family did not treat her as disabled and she was mainstreamed throughout her education—college and a graduate degree. She then landed an executive position in the retail garment business, became a production manager and traveled to China, Thailand, Turkey and the Philippines, among other countries, to negotiate and supervise factory production. The factory managers, she says, when they first saw her, were not only shocked to meet a woman executive but also a woman who "walks crazy." "I think I scared the hell out of them," she says. But, "It ended up working out. People understood." Her clients respected her expertise and her company's financial power. She loved her work and was very successful, making a salary of six figures.

Molly met her husband in Columbus, Ohio, where her company sent her from Los Angeles where she had started her job. She says they met at a bar and he asked her for a date. She was surprised and a little annoyed when on the date he asked, "What's up with the way you are walking?" She thought he'd noticed the way she walked when they first met. They talked about it and though it took a while before they developed a relationship, they became engaged and married. His family welcomed her warmly.

Before they decided to have children, Molly and her husband went to a genetic counselor. The counselor reviewed the options open to them. If they didn't want to have children on their own, they could adopt. Or they could go to a fertility clinic and use an egg donor. She says they explored the latter option but felt that it was not only very expensive but also presented other issues, such as the possibility of getting an egg donor with some other kind of problem—type two diabetes, for instance. They reasoned that "it was scarier to take on the unknown rather than something we already knew." They decided to have their own child.

Molly notes that today a woman with HSP would be offered a third option. Because so much more is known about genes, scientists now can know exactly what gene mutation a parent with HSP has and can find out after a pregnancy begins if the child is going to have the disability. The woman would have the option to terminate the pregnancy. Though that would not be the option Molly and her husband would have chosen, she feels everyone has to make their own choice. "Some people can really handle it [knowing the child will have a disability] and some people can not," she says, and she continues, "Everyone has to know what they can deal with and go with that."

Molly: You know, I hate to tell you but he really does have HSP

The definite diagnosis that her son had HSP occurred around their son's second birthday. He was having some persistent balance issues in walking so they took him to his pediatrician to check it out. The doctor said, "You know,

I hate to tell you, but he really does have HSP." Her husband's reaction was completely unexpected. He started arguing and demanding an MRI even though the doctor insisted, "You're really denying what is here in front of you." Molly recalls that he became lightheaded and woozy and had to sit down. Afterward, she says. "There were just weeks and weeks of pure trauma." She remembers that when they went over to his parents' house for dinner and they were saying the dinner prayer "his father, you know, would just burst into tears."

"I went as far as getting counseling for my entire extended family—my father-in-law, my mother-in-law, my sister in-law," Molly says, "because no one was talking about it when I was around. But, they *were* talking about it. My husband was having secret meetings with his mother at lunch. And they were journaling and were keeping it all to themselves. And I was like this is crazy." She felt that her husband was going to leave. She was pregnant with their second child and she remembers, "I felt it was just going to be me and Rhys and this unborn baby. It was really rough."

I asked Molly what had pulled them through. In time, she says, they have become a real family. When I interviewed Molly, it was the beginning of summer and school was out and she and her husband and the two boys were enjoying the chance to spend some time together. "We've gone to the pool almost every day she says, "We're really together. It's been fantastic." She adds, "What got us through all our trials and tribulations has just been totally being in love with one another. It's this deep love that the four of us have."

The fourth family member is their second son, Liam, born two years after Rhys. He does not have HSP and has seemed at times "like a super baby," she says. She has had to get used to the fact of his agility and speed. When Rhys was learning to ride a bike with training wheels at six, Molly walked slowly beside him, but when Liam took his turn on the bike, he was at the end of the block instantly, almost out of sight. They decided his father would be the one to take him for bike rides!

Rhys has more physical challenges than his mother had. He wears braces and has to have botox injections periodically, requiring a trip to Cincinnati to see a specialist. At times, Molly says she feels responsible for her son's disability. She feels as if she's "done this to this person in a weird kind of way." She talks to Rick about HSP and shares any new information that comes up about it. When he got a pair of braces, she got a pair for herself, thinking they might help her, too, but also to make her feel more identified with his experience.

Molly and her husband enrolled Rhys in a parochial school in their neighborhood despite the fact that this private school did not have access to federally supported special education programs. Rhys has done well at his school. He has excelled academically and is nicknamed fondly "the Mayor" because he is so outgoing and knows everyone's first and last names. Although they have to supplement the school program with physical therapy and have to make special arrangements for physical education classes, Molly says they are very happy with the school. The principal and the teachers treat Rhys like all the other children but they are also supportive of any special needs that he has.

Molly: I think people are more willing to tell me what their problems are, because they know I have them, too

Molly and her husband wrote a letter to every student in his school when he first went, telling them about his disability and saying they welcomed any questions about it. The response was wonderful, she says. "We got some beautiful little notes from the children's parents saying what a brave thing to do and thanking us for sharing this. They said they'd talked to their children and they totally embraced us." What was even more moving, Molly says, was the way her openness encouraged many families to share their own problems with her:

> Almost every single family has some thing going on. That's really been an eye opener. I looked at everyone as having these perfect genes! And they really don't. They have learning disabilities, they have leukemia or lymphoma and these are all just children! I didn't think that there were so many disabilities out there. It seems like one out of three families have some kind of issue.

She found that many parents were glad to be able to share their problems with someone. "I think people are more willing to tell me what their problems are, because they know I have them, too. " Molly says, and acknowledges she has a deeper understanding of herself as a disabled parent.

Molly has been changed—as many people are—by becoming a mother. She says that her career used to define her and she does not regret that. She kept working until her second son was born, but now feels she would not go back to the same kind of demanding career, though it took her a while to accept the role of just a "stay at home" mom. Although she knows she will do some kind of work again, she has definitely become more engaged in issues of disability and particularly those concerning mothers with disabilities. About being a mother, she says, "It's been so rewarding and fulfilling."

In her experience of deciding to have a child despite the possibility of passing on her genetic disability, Molly faced some tough issues. The reaction to her son's diagnosis was unexpected and shocking to her, particularly since her disability had not prevented her from having a successful and full life. Eventually her husband's family was able to broaden their understanding of disability and fully accept and love their grandson. Molly also gained a new perception about disability. By reaching out to the parents at her son's school, she found that almost all families experienced some kind of problem that could be defined as a disability and that they were eager to share them with her.

No doubt many women and many couples who plan to have children are not even aware of the genetic question though medical science is making more and more information available to us about our genetic code. Women or parents with disabilities who know, however, that they might have a particular genetic disability, like Molly and her husband, might choose to consult a genetic counselor. Laura and her husband knew they wanted to do some genetic testing when they decided to have children, and they started with a different premise about the possibility of passing on a genetic disability to their child.

Laura: We knew we'd be happy in helping to shape and guide a young person along life's path

Laura and her husband are both of short stature (dwarfism). Far from being worried or anxious about having a child inherit their disability, they actually looked forward to sharing their experience and knowledge. Of course, Laura adds, they knew they had a chance of having an "average" child, which would also be an exciting challenge. In either case, she says they would be happy in "helping to shape and guide a young person along life's path."

Both Laura, who is thirty-eight, and her husband come from "average" sized families. All of their siblings and nieces and nephews are of average size so as potential parents, they were charting an unfamiliar course. Because each of them has a different kind of dwarfism, they did not know the outcome if both recessive genes were passed onto the child. Laura says "There really aren't any recorded statistics—no documented research—of what would be the outcome of a couple with different types of dwarfism having a child." They knew that they would want to do some genetic testing.

Laura was in a very good position to follow up all she needed to know about the genetics of their child and to plan her pregnancy. She has an undergraduate degree in biology and a graduate degree in health care management and her career has been in health care in an HMO. As a scientist, she had the interest and the training to understand the risks of her pregnancy and to examine her options carefully. She put together a genetic team, some of whom were familiar with her as a guest lecturer in some of their medical school classes. At the same time, she also engaged a high risk pregnancy team so, as she said, "they would be comfortable taking on a woman with a short stature and possibly delivering a child with dwarfism as well." All of this was pre-pregnancy, including genetic testing on her husband to confirm his type of dwarfism since he had never had a full diagnosis done. Laura agrees she was unusually well prepared and foresighted. "That's just who I am…that's what is comfortable for me," she says.

Their plan was to do genetic testing when Laura was pregnant to find out what kind of dwarfism the child would have, if any. It was important to know if there was double dominance—having both type of genes—because then it was unlikely that the child would survive outside the womb because of severe or lethal skeletal dysplasia. Also they needed more information to know how to handle the pregnancy. If her husband's dwarfism was passed on, it would be a bigger baby with a bigger head, and that would have taken a little more planning for the pregnancy and delivery since Laura is very small. Finding the right genetic labs to do the testing was challenging. Most labs just test for one type of dwarfism but over a period of two weeks and many calls and interviews, Laura found the lab she could trust and the genetic counseling team there that she could consult. After they sent the CVS (chorionic villi) sample cultures, they had to wait about four weeks for the results. Laura and her husband didn't tell his parents about the testing until after it was completed, fearing it would make them nervous, but Laura's' parents were informed about the process because they were more familiar with the plan and knew that Laura and Therin were comfortable with it.

Laura says that she and her husband knew that "they would be able to handle whatever was going to come our way," but they were excited when the call came from the lab's genetic counseling team. As is customary, the technician asked to speak to the female partner, but Laura arranged a conference call so that she and her husband could hear the results together. They were told that it was a girl and that she had Laura's type of dwarfism. They were thrilled! Laura thought it was interesting that the director of the genetic lab was relieved that she and her husband were pleased. More commonly, he found that parents would be upset to hear the news that their child would be born with a disability.

Laura: I don't think I'm your average everyday c-section patient

Laura's' pregnancy went well and her medical team, which was familiar with high risk pregnancies, monitored her carefully and made sure she carried her baby to full term. She had a c-section and a spinal. She says, "My tolerance for pain is high. I didn't even need any pain medication for this procedure." But she added, "I don't think I'm your average everyday c-section patient. I wasn't uncomfortable at all." Always the scientist, Laura was also pleased to be part of a medical research study that was examining the best type of anesthesia for women of short stature.

Not surprisingly, Laura and her husband did a lot of pre-planning before they took their daughter home. They had a lower changing table and a convertible stroller and made needed household modifications. Laura was able to nurse Katie Mae for fifteen months after some help from a lactation nurse who came to the house. She and her husband shared in the tasks of dressing and bathing and carrying. They decided that she would work full time and her husband would switch his career to part-time. Katie Mae goes to daycare three days a week and she is home with her father the other two days.

Laura has a very optimistic attitude about parenting with a disability. But in her interview, she adds, "You should probably know about my husband and me. We are very open and transparent about our limitations and our disability. To some people we can seem overly positive. To other people it can be motivating. So I just frame it to say, 'This is just our personal experience and how we handle our life and our challenges.'"

Laura: It's the most rewarding job I've had… I'm just so glad I've had this opportunity to be a mother

More specifically, about her role as a mother, Laura says, "There are some things I'm going to be very good at and then there are some things I will need a lot of help with. It's just setting realistic expectations of myself and what I can provide for her [Katie Mae] and how my husband can co-manage." She knows things will continue to change and she knows she is going to continue to be a good problem solver. However, her feelings about being a mother will not change. She says, "It is the most rewarding job I've had and I'm just so glad I've had this opportunity to be a mother. Sometimes, it's still hard for me to say, 'Oh, I'm a mother,' because I just can't believe I have this amazing responsibility."

When asked if they plan to have more children, Laura says, "Yes, we are hoping to" and she reflects that it might be a different experience. They could have a child of average size and "that would be another opportunity to guide and help develop someone."

Of five women interviewed who potentially could pass on their genetic disability, the message was clear that the genetic question should not deter a disabled person from having children. As one mother, who has rheumatoid arthritis said, "I thought about that and then I said 'Is that such a tragedy? I don't think I'm that bad.'" Four of the women consulted genetic counselors and one, Laura, took the next step and had genetic testing. Molly said she would not choose to use the current technology, which would enable her to know if her baby would have her disability and potentially enable her to choose not to have the child.

The question of genetic testing and its relationship to selective abortion has been a much discussed topic, increasingly controversial, as technological advancements increase. The biologist and feminist Ruth Hubbard expressed her concern about prenatal testing and its potential negative effect on the reproductive rights of women with disabilities. She argues that a woman must have a choice about terminating a pregnancy but that she should also expect society to support her decision to have the child if she chooses. In *The Politics of Biology (1997)* she writes:

> So once more, yes, a woman must have the right to terminate a pregnancy, whatever her reasons, but she must also feel empowered not to terminate it, confident that the society will do what it can to enable her and her child to have fulfilling lives. To the extent that prenatal interventions implement social prejudices against people with disabilities they do not expand our reproductive rights. They constrict them. (p. 199)

2. ADOPTION AS AN ALTERNATIVE

Denise: Suddenly I found myself the mother I had always dreamed about

When Molly and her husband consulted a genetic counselor, he pointed out that one option for them was adopting a child so that they would be sure that she would not pass on her HSP gene. Neither Molly nor any of the women interviewed chose adoption over giving birth, but two of the women adopted children after they gave birth. One adopted two brothers and another adopted two boys and is guardian to a third. Additionally, one mother, who lost a twin girl in the birth of her son, said she would like to adopt a daughter in the future. In *The Question of David: A Disabled Mother's Journey Through Adoption, Family and Life* (1999), Denise Sherer Jacobsen shares the process of adoption and the troubles and joys that she and her husband experienced. She recounts the familiar prejudice toward disability that they encountered when they applied to adopt a four month old baby boy, whose birth mother put him up for adoption because he was disabled. Denise, who has cerebral palsy as does her husband, describes her journey to Saint Louis to meet the baby and two wonderful women whose mission is to place children for adoption, particularly if they are disabled. When permission for temporary custody was finally given, Denise, who was going to be the primary caregiver, faced a negative attitude from both her own family and from some doctors. When told of the news of the adoption, her mother-in-law said, "What do you want a sick baby for?" And when Denise and her husband received the required medical form from their doctor, they were disturbed that he had written, "Couple's cerebral palsy presents a potential hazard in raising a child." They changed doctors and after a thorough exam and consultation, this doctor gave them a positive recommendation. In the rest of her account, Denise describes the challenges and successes of the following months and years of caring for David. At one point, she describes the impact that motherhood has had on her. It has fulfilled an improbable dream but it also has taught her to trust her intuition and instincts. Her sentiments echo some of the feeling of the women interviewed. She writes:

> *For perhaps the first time in my life, I was the center of someone's world; not as a burden, but as a protector. Suddenly I found myself the mother I had often dreamed about. David had thrust me into my now cherished role, one that demanded use of all my resources and strengths... I had to learn to trust myself. That trust, which would prove so crucial in mothering a child, had been buried within me for such a long time* (pp.182-83).

3. CHOOSING MOTHERHOOD: HOW WE ARE SEEN

The other women I interviewed did not have hereditary disabilities. As Adrienne Asch (1997) has written, "The vast majority of disabilities are not hereditary (p.248)." But, as she further notes, that does not always prevent a negative attitude toward a disabled woman's pregnancy by the medical world, resulting sometimes in medical professionals urging or coercing women into being sterilized or, as other studies have shown, urging the women to terminate the pregnancy (Prilleltensky, 2003). Other women experience being advised by medical professionals to put their child up for adoption. assuming that they cannot be trustworthy mothers. When Lilly found that the doctors and counselors in the rehabilitation hospital just assumed that she would put her baby up for adoption because of her spinal cord injury, she recalls," I was more determined to prove the doctors, the medical team and especially society wrong."

Sometimes a disabled woman must face negativity from both her public and private worlds. In an essay from *Bigger than the Sky: Disabled Women on Parenting (1999),* Jo Litwinowiz, who was born with cerebral palsy and uses a wheelchair, couldn't find anyone to share her and her husband's excitement at the prospect of their having a child. They knew it would be a challenge, but they knew they could be good parents. At her first appointment with her obstetrician, he told her that she could have an abortion any time during her pregnancy and urged her to go home and think about it. The next day a woman from Family Planning came to her house and told her she couldn't possibly raise a child in her condition and when her child became aware that she was different from other mothers, he would resent her and tell her he wanted a "new mother." Her husband promptly showed the woman the door. As if all this negativity were not enough, this expectant disabled mother found that when she called her parents to let them know the good news, she received silence from her mother and a rebuke from her father who said, "Well, Jo, that news has turned this day into a tragic day. You are an irresponsible and stupid girl" (p. 31).

Some of this negative attitude toward disabled women becoming mothers grows from the perception that they are defective as women, particularly regarding their sexuality. The Center for Research on Women (CROWD) (2009) at Baylor University concludes that "Women with disabilities report that medical professionals often regard them as being asexual." This attitude can often translate into seeing women with disabilities as incapable of conceiving and bearing a child and of being mothers. Sometimes, these prejudices, as part of the culture, are reflected in the family and parents of women with disabilities. Compare Talia's story with Chris's, whose family were supportive and positive about her becoming a mother.

Talia: I'd been constantly told throughout my life that I was unable to take care of myself, so how could I take care of someone else?

Talia, born in 1973 with cerebral palsy, uses crutches and a wheelchair. She says that her mother never talked to her about her reproductive or sexual life; she found out about birth control pills from her doctor. Actually, studies show that able bodied women also seldom discuss sexuality issues with their family and usually get their information from books or their doctors. Most girls and young women grow up with the expectation that they will marry and have children, but Talia's mother never talked to her about having children. In fact, she avoided the subject. Talia's family, for the most part, also had a negative attitude toward her disability. She says, "My father didn't like the fact that I had a disability. He thought it was my fault that I didn't try to walk enough." He could not accept her impairments so he tried to push her to make them better. Her maternal grandmother, Talia says, "right from the get-go wanted to have me put away in an institution" and her family's house was never made accessible to meet her needs. "So I had to learn to live in the society in which we live," as she put it. This negativity from her family, an example of the ableism so prevalent in much of society that can't accept the differences of the person with a disability, affected Talia's perception of herself as a young woman and as a possible mother.

Talia does add that her mother was supportive in some ways, particularly as an advocate for her in her school years. She kept her out of Special Education classes, which would have demoted her academically. "The school automatically thought that because I have a physical disability, I must have a limited mental capacity." With her mother's support, she continued to fight throughout her high school years to be treated like everyone else. They got accommodations from the school, such as keeping a set of her subject books in each of her classrooms so that she could be independent and did not have an aide assigned to carry her books. Talia graduated successfully and went on to receive a B.S. from Bridgewater State College.

Despite Talia's achievements, her family's negative attitude undermined her self-confidence and her perception of herself and she initially felt discouraged about becoming a mother. She says, "I'd been constantly told throughout my life that I'm unable to take care of myself, so how could I take care of someone else? I didn't really seriously think I could do it." Her husband, who also has cerebral palsy, did think they could become parents but because of her uncertainty, they put off any decision. Then Talia discovered she was pregnant. She was shocked! Her doctor had told her she no longer needed birth control pills because she has polycystic ovaries that would prevent conception. "I was scared to death," she says, "and scared throughout my whole pregnancy."

Talia credits her friends, particularly those she met from the United Cerebral Palsy Association, for getting her through many tough spots and convincing her that if they could have children successfully, so could she. Her pregnancy went well and she gave birth with a cesarean to a healthy baby girl.

Talia: I had post partum depression and I was really sad

When she returned home, Talia needed a lot of support. She and her husband had just moved into a new house and they were both overwhelmed. Talia says she was rescued by the Doula Program, a private service that trains women to provide help to new mothers in their labor, birth and the post partum period. A doula came to her home to help her through many of the first demanding steps of infant care. She was helped with breast feeding and shown how she could adapt to manage many tasks such as changing diapers and dressing and bathing her child. In addition, the doula did some of the household chores and shopping. "She also helped me through a lot of the emotional part," Talia says: "I had post partum depression and I was really sad." Her mother tried to be helpful but was unable to accept the fact that Talia was experiencing a common post childbirth condition of depression and kept telling her that she needed to "get up and get moving." Also she could not understand Talia's adaptations in caring for the infant and insisted that she do things "the right way."

After her doula left, Talia still felt overwhelmed at times and contacted Social Services for a short term counselor who could come to the house. That experience was not a good one, The woman spent very little time listening to her and drew irrelevant conclusions, including a suggestion that she should leave the marriage. Talia remembers she was really taken aback and thought "Lady, you haven't met me for five minutes, who are you to say who I am?" She concludes, "I guess this kind of snap judgment is not unusual, but it is ignorance I suppose."

Since Talia is herself a social worker and counsels disabled mothers at the Springfield Community Access Program, she is particularly disturbed by the failings of the social service system, which can be ineffectual because of inflexible rules and short-sighted responses. For instance, Talia thinks there should be parenting classes for disabled mothers but fears that if child welfare services got involved, it could jump to the inappropriate conclusion that the mothers were unfit to take care of their children.

Talia: I may do it differently, but I know I can take care of her

With the help of her friends who are disabled mothers and her husband, who shares the care giving and house hold tasks, Talia has overcome much of the apprehension that made becoming a mother more difficult than it should have been. Her peers have convinced her that she can take care of her daughter. She says "I may do it differently, but I know I can take care of her and that she loves me and bonds with me." Talia and her husband compensate for one another and their different kinds of impairments. His speech is more impaired but he can walk and drive. He cooks and she cleans and they share childcare at home and take Emily to day care daily.

Talia: Really, it's changed my life for the better

Becoming a mother has changed Talia's self-image. "Really, it's changed my life for the better," she says. "It's been an eye-opener for me and a confidence builder, because I realize that I can do it. You have to be very persistent and have a lot of perseverance. And you have to be very independent and determined. I just might not do it anyone else's way, but it's my way. And it's making us a closer family unit as well."

Talia now looks forward to having a second child. She says, "I know how I'm going to do it differently this time. Now I'm going into it with a whole different mindset, that's changed from 'I can't do it.' Now it's just 'when do I want to do it?'"

Chris: Ever since I was a kid being a mother was always one of my goals

In contrast to Talia, Chris, who is thirty-nine and has Juvenile Rheumatoid Arthritis, has a family who have always been supportive of her being a mother. She says, "My mom thinks everyone should have children and everybody should have twins." Chris has a twin sister and she had twin boys. She explains:

> *Ever since I was a kid, it [being a mother] was always one of my goals. Even though I knew I had arthritis and would be in and out of wheelchairs, that was*

always part of my plan—to have a family and have children, whatever that meant. It was never a question, it was always just natural for me always to be a mom.

Chris uses a scooter now though she was in a wheelchair after hip replacements earlier in her life. Her arthritis and its pain can flare up periodically, but, as Chris says, it was in remission during and sometime after her pregnancy.

Chris definitely had a plan about becoming a mother. She didn't consider her disability a deterring factor, though she had to think about it, she says. She acknowledged that she might pass on the arthritis but felt that wasn't such a tragedy. First, she knew she would need extra help and had to plan her support system. She lived in her mother's house and had friends and relatives, including her twin sister, whom she knew would be willing to help her. Then she wanted to be sure she was physically able to be pregnant and give birth. Her surgeon. who had done her hip replacements, said, "Make sure if you get pregnant, you have a c-section." And her rheumatologist didn't see pregnancy as a problem. But above all, she remembers thinking, "I had to get a guy—that's kind of important!"

Chris met the right man, Matt, who has psoriatic arthritis. Neither of them had had a serious relationship before they met. They were together a while before they got married but Chris didn't wait too long to feel him out about his interest in having a family. She describes how the subject evolved:

I think it was the six month time line. I started asking some questions: well, do you want a family? Just sort of so I could know if we were on the same page. And I remember he wasn't actually 100% sure and I was somewhat like that too, but I knew I needed a good supportive husband. It just evolved for him as we developed a relationship and got married. Then it was a natural thing for him.

Her immediate family, Chris says, was 90% supportive about their decision to have children. Some of the family members on both sides were not as supportive. They thought it was selfish: "How dare we bring a child into this world with the possibility of having arthritis?" She and Matt responded, "What is that saying about us?" She continues, "I think a lot of people just assumed I wouldn't be able to carry a child so they were shocked and surprised."

Chris was 37 when she got married and a year later they consulted her doctor because they were anxious to have a child. He suggested that she and Matt get tested for infertility because of "my advanced age!" They got tested and found that neither of them had a problem; the diagnosis was "unexplained infertility." After some hesitation, they decided to try fertility treatments. They had heard stories of long arduous treatments for infertility that sometimes ended in failure, but they decided they were ready to accept whatever happened. Fortunately, after the second round of intrauterine insemination. Chris became pregnant. When the blood work came back, they were told the numbers were high so they could expect more than one baby. Since both Chris and Matt had twins in their family, they were prepared for twins but began to worry it might be triplets!

Chris: Oh my God, just let there be two!

At six weeks they went and had an ultrasound. Chris describes the moment. "Matt had to sit down. I was thinking, 'Oh my god, just let there be two.' The technician didn't say anything after we saw the second heart beat. Matt asked, "Is there another one hiding there? And the technician said no, just two." My mother and aunt were with us and Chris says, "They were ecstatic. They were out of their minds. My mother wishes twins on everybody. Apparently she wished them on me too. Matt and I were just numb but we were excited, too."

Chris's pregnancy was not too difficult, she says. She was able to use her scooter during the pregnancy until she became too big to fit behind the steering wheel. She only gained twenty-six pounds, which was good considering she was carrying twins. She did have some "rocky periods" and had to have bed rest for preterm contractions but that didn't last long. Most importantly, her doctor, a woman, was wonderful, she says, and willing to be in touch, giving her advice about what kind of activities she could handle. She knew beforehand that her delivery would be with a c-section because of her hip replacements and that she would have a local and be awake as she had been for all of her surgeries. The procedure seemed very short to her compared to the long orthopedic procedures she had gone through in the past.

Chris: I've been improvising since I knew what the word meant

As always, Chris had planned and thought ahead about how she would take care of her twin babies—how she would hold them, carry them, change their diapers and clothes and feed and bathe them. Everything was set up for her before she came home from the hospital so she didn't have to go up and down stairs. She remembers at first she was nervous. "For the first three weeks, I didn't want to be alone at all, maybe for an hour until I knew what I could do for them. Now I have no problem. If they are both screaming, that's all right; one has to wait. I manage. I make do." She breast feeds both but with supplemental bottles, which, she says, she is using more often. She can usually change diapers and give sponge baths and dress them though snaps can be a challenge for her hands so a cousin has sewn Velcro on many of the clothes. Chris knows how to improvise. As she says, "I've been improvising since I knew what the word meant. For me it's just natural."

With adaptations and improvisations, Chris feels she can do much of the care giving, but she also acknowledges that she needs a lot of help and has been fortunate in having it. Her mother is always available in the same house and her siblings, particularly her twin sister, often come to help her out. A neighbor comes over every day and she has helpers who come in daily to assist her in carrying out some of the tasks of caring for her babies, especially taking on one of the twins while she is attending to the other. Of course, as Chris says, Matt, her husband, does a great deal, too, after he comes home from work every day. He cooks dinner and does laundry and bottles and other chores. Chris would someday like to have her own home and have a kitchen which she could manage herself and do some cooking and laundry. But for the time being, she accomplishes the household tasks and care giving with help and planning. As she says, "It's doable."

Chris: Plan things out…even if you know it may work out differently

When asked about her advice to other women who want to have children, Chris emphasizes planning, which she does so well. She says, "Plan things out, if you're not a plan person, try to make a plan even if you know it may work out differently. Do your research. If you're not fortunate to have a lot of support, think ahead and utilize what you can. Call your local high school—kids are looking for community service, call your church—they often have volunteers—call your neighbor, who might have a teenager who wants to be hired as a mother's helper." She goes on to say, "Also just know that you are going to do the best you can. Just because you have a disability, don't let that be a negative."

Becoming a mother has been the realization for Chris of a goal she has had for a long time: to become a mother before she was forty. She made it three months before the deadline, she says! She feels it was just the right time for her to have children. She says, "I think I'm much more prepared now than I would have been five or ten years ago—I'm more relaxed, less stressed." Chris's twins are just three months old. She says, "I know all this is going to be interesting when they get older. I know there will be many challenges, but so far I've managed and I'm doing much better than I ever thought I could."

Phouvieng: I didn't expect to raise my daughters by myself

Although several other women interviewed had strong encouragement and support from their families when they were deciding whether to have a child, others, like Talia and Jo Litwinowicz did not. An extreme example of lack of support is Phouvieng's story. She is an immigrant from Laos, who had contracted polio at the age of one because no vaccine was available. In 1979, when she was five, her entire family, including five brothers and two sisters, escaped from Laos after the country's civil war by swimming across the river to Thailand. One of her brothers swam with Phouvieng on his shoulders. Phouvieng says, "We stayed in [an IDP] camp for a year until we got a visa for America." They eventually settled in the Laotian community of Wichita, Kansas.

Formerly an officer in the Laotian army, Phouvieng's father, she says, was abusive. Once in America, her mother left him and took the family to live with a cousin. Growing up, Phouvieng's mother and siblings were ashamed of her disability and saw it as an imperfection that was unacceptable and should be hidden. Her family rarely spoke about her disability, Phouvieng says. She thinks that this was part of a cultural bias that included her mother's conviction that she would never marry. Her mother never acknowledged her daughter's pregnancy. She eventually returned to Laos, returning only once to Wichita.

Phouvieng: I was the most Americanized

Feeling very much on her own as she grew up, Phouvieng pursued her own path. "I was the most Americanized," she said of her family. Her polio had affected her growth and left her with severe scoliosis, which was not properly treated when she was a child. Despite her disability, she was able to be very mobile with crutches. She worked hard in school and got scholarships to the University of Wichita where she did well and was even part of the crew team. She met her children's father at the university. When she became pregnant, she had no support from family or the Laotian community. Though her "common law husband" was "a little bit helpful for the first year" he was mostly off working and training for the military. Phouvieng left him just before her second daughter's first birthday. She now receives Social Security Disability Insurance (SSDI) and sporadic child support.

Phouvieng's experience with the medical world during her pregnancy and delivery was mixed. When she was first pregnant, she saw an intern, who was both uninformed and unhelpful. Phouvieng says, "She told me I had a high risk for a miscarriage and she didn't know if the baby was going to be deformed or what was going to happen." Although her pregnancy was fairly normal, she had a number of falls as she grew heavier and had balance problems. "I fell so many times. It was just unbelievable." She began to use a wheelchair. Both deliveries were by cesareans though the doctor considered a natural delivery for her second child. However, he was not sure how her disability might affect the delivery—whether her pelvic bone was wide enough—and so she had a c-section.

Phouvieng says, "I didn't expect to raise my daughters by myself," but she has done just that. Neither her family or the Laotian community were supportive. She was not even successful in getting help from social services. When struggling to care for a toddler and an infant, she contacted a state agency to inquire about home aid.

> *I called social services and the Women's Center in Wichita when I was preg-*
> *nant with my second child. I asked if they could send somebody to come and*
> *help me out [with childcare or household chores]. The man [who took the call]*
> *told me they could not—that they could only deal with people who aren't able*
> *to care for themselves.*

Ironically, Phouvieng was not disabled *enough* to get the social services that could help her be a better mother. And, as the availability of such services varies regionally, in some states, including Kansas, childcare is excluded from the personal care assistance available to adults who qualify as disabled.

Phouvieng wanted very much to finish her college degree, but found the obstacles insurmountable. "I tried to go to classes when I was pregnant with my second child, but I didn't have anyone to watch the baby so I took her to class with me," explains Phouvieng, "but they told me I couldn't bring her."

Phouvieng's remarkable ingenuity characterizes her story of survival. When she was pregnant the second time, she had no car and only a three-wheel scooter. In order to go grocery shopping, a mile or so away, she had to tie Erika, then under two, in a car seat to the back of her scooter: "I had to drive that in the winter…to strap my daughter in the car seat on my scooter so she didn't fall off. And I had to stand [while driving]." When the three of them go food shopping now they take a bus, sometimes waiting for as long as an hour, and they carry a backpack on wheels to bring the food home. Sometimes they have to make several trips to finish shopping.

Phouvieng credits her success in care giving and in managing her household to her strict scheduling. She had the toddlers on rigid sleeping schedules, giving her time to do household chores and she taught them to obey her, a practice familiar in her own cultural tradition. Her first daughter, Erika, was well behaved and obedient. If Phouvieng had to discipline her, she says, "I just grabbed her by the arms, you know gently, and talked to her and said 'no, you don't do that.' Then I put her in Time Out." Ellen, the second child, who is more mischievous, nevertheless follows the pattern Phouvieng established. Now that they are older, they each have chores to do. Phouvieng says, "I'm teaching them to be independent. They have to do their share of the work."

Although her daughters were isolated in their family unit for a long time, they are very understanding, loving and caring about other people. Phouvieng says she wants them to "not judge other people." They are also protective of her if friends or classmates tease them about their mother's short stature and call her a midget. Phouvieng is four feet, three inches tall and has been mistaken more than once for her daughters' sister. She feels the attitude hasn't bothered the girls and that they just try to educate the other children. She started to talk to them about her disability when her youngest daughter at age eight saw a boy with crutches and began to ask questions. She herself is connecting more with her children's school and plans to do workshops on disability there, talking about her life and emphasizing what she *can do* more than what she cannot do.

Phouvieng's aspiration for her daughters is for them "to be the best that they can be." She also wants them to be able to take care of themselves. She knows from her own hard times that you just have to keep going and she tells them that if you fail at something, "It's not the end of the world. If it doesn't work for you at that time, just try something else." She encourages other women with disabilities to have children but warns that "it can be tough" and that they should be prepared, emotionally, financially and practically. As for herself, she says, being a mother is very rewarding. She has a special bond with her daughters. She says, "There's a bond. I mean it's just amazing!"

As these women's stories illustrate, deciding to have a child challenges their physical and emotional identity. They face many issues: whether or not they will pass on their disability genetically or whether they can become pregnant, or as in Talia's case, whether she can overcome her fear and anxiety about the responsibility of having a child. When they chose to become mothers, these women experienced very different kinds of reactions from their families—from very supportive to hostile to indifferent—but all of them reaffirmed their decision to become mothers and found that they had been empowered.

4. PREGNANCY AND WORKING WITH THE MEDICAL ESTABLISHMENT

The five women profiled in the stories above were fortunate in having relatively easy pregnancies and deliveries. Four of them had cesareans because of the particular conditions of their disabilities although it is not clear whether or not Phouvieng could have delivered naturally if her doctor had known more about her disability. Molly had vaginal deliveries for both of her sons.

According to Judy Norsigian (2009), executive director *of Our Bodies Ourselves*, one-third of all US women deliver their babies by caesarean section, which, she says is a rate "that is far higher than medically necessary." (The Boston Globe A11). About half of the twenty-five women interviewed here had caesarean sections. In most cases, those who had c-sections agreed that they were necessary because of their disability. Several, however, felt they were not adequately consulted and perhaps could have chosen vaginal deliveries. The obstetricians involved were often uninformed about the way the disability might affect the delivery. This lack of knowledge was true about the relationship to the women's reproductive health in general.

In almost a collective voice in the interviews, the women said that in their experience, doctors and health professionals do not know enough, if anything, about their particular disability and how it can affect their pregnancy or delivery or their post partum health. Research from CROWD supports this when they report: "Primary care physicians and obstetrician/gynecologists generally receive very little if any training in the effect of disability on the reproductive health of women" (CROWD, 2009).

As one woman says about her pregnancy, labor and postpartum experience, "It was a new experience for them [doctors and healthcare professionals]. Another says about her doctor, "He had no idea how I would take to pregnancy." And another had a further comment: "Doctors only have five minutes or fifteen minutes of disability training. And I think they need more. And I think they need more sensitivity training."

Becky: I had to be my own [medical] manager

Becky's story is an example of the need for doctors to have more specific knowledge about the effects of a particular disability on a disabled women's reproductive health. Becky, who was born in 1961 and has multiple sclerosis, found that her doctors and nurses lacked an understanding of her disability during her pregnancies, deliveries and postpartum experiences. She has two daughters. Her doctors—a gynecologist and neurologist—didn't communicate with one another and as Becky says, "I had to be my own manager."

During our interview, Becky spoke several times about cognitive difficulties she was experiencing; occasionally, she would stop and reorient herself in the conversation, saying, "See, that's what I mean. I've forgotten the question." But her lapses did not diminish her keen mind and the witty, somewhat satirical, narrative of her experiences.

First of all, she explains, her neurologist wanted to try an experimental chemotherapy treatment on her MS but warned that it would make her menopausal and hence sterile. Becky, who was then twenty-five, objected that she wanted to have children. She relates the conversation. "The doctor said, 'Well start having children.' And I said 'Well, I thought I had to be married before I had kids.' And he said, 'Well, go get married.'"

Becky insists that as the result of this conversation, she immediately looked for a husband and got married! She says, "I married the first [husband] I could find, who was willing. He turned out to be a total jerk." They had two daughters and two years after her second child was born, she divorced and has since married again. She says of her second husband, "He's wonderful. More than anyone else who doesn't have MS, I believe he has an inkling of the truth about what it must be like for me. Certainly he has just the right combination of knowing when to help and knowing when to rejoice in my independence."

Her first birth was induced over a period of three days and, as Becky explains, she doesn't have much sensation below her thighs, so she did not feel her contractions though she felt shivery, feverish and "as if I was doing something terribly difficult." After her water broke on the third day at two p.m., the midwife in attendance told Becky she would deliver about midnight. Becky was sure she was closer to delivering and asked the nurse to check her. After arguing with her, the midwife finally did check her and quickly called for help. The baby was born at four twenty.

Becky had a similar experience with the birth of her second daughter. This pregnancy and delivery was even more complicated. At twenty-seven weeks into the pregnancy, fearing a premature birth, the doctors, without consulting a neurologist, put her into a high risk natal unit and prescribed almost complete bed rest for six and a half weeks. This inactivity combined with the regular steroids she took was very harmful to her MS, weakening her bones. When she finally was induced at thirty-six weeks, the doctors and nurses again did not understand the way her lack of sensation affected her labor. She was at a different hospital this time. After she was induced, the nurse told her to push. Becky could not feel whether or not she was pushing, but she says she tried something that she imagined was a push. Then the nurse told her to stop pushing. By this time the baby actually started to crown, which sent everyone rushing for the doctor, who had left for lunch, thinking the labor would continue for several hours.

Becky: Nobody is stronger than spasticity

The consequences of the steroids and bed rest showed up when her newborn was five days old and Becky broke her ankle when she had a fall at home. Her bones were very thin and brittle. A friend drove her to the emergency room—her husband, she says, was unwilling—and Becky took the infant with her. Once again she found doctors unfamiliar with her condition. An x-ray showed a fracture and the doctor said he would give her a cast. Becky tried to explain that the spasticity in her leg was very strong and would resist a cast, but she recalls that the doctor said, I can make a cast that's stronger than your spasticity." As it turned out, he couldn't. As Becky comments, "Nobody is stronger than spasticity." When she went to her regular orthopedist, she found that the ankle had broken again and she needed surgery.

The end of that episode, Becky continues, is that they couldn't find an immediate surgery date and so she went to her sister's wedding, which was in Italy, with a leg splint and in a rented wheel chair. She says, "I don't know what my mother did to get me on the plane. My mother may have bribed the captain. She's capable of anything. So I went to Italy with a newborn baby, a three and a half year old, a surly husband, two brothers and a mother."

Becky had the surgery when she returned and afterwards had two years of trouble with the pressure sore on her heel that came from the original cast. She eventually had to have more surgery to release her heel cord. She also had the chemotherapy that she had put off to have children. She did go into menopause though her general doctor at first refused to believe that it was possible for her to be menopausal at thirty-nine. I asked Becky if the chemotherapy had helped her MS and she says, "Not really." So the great rush to get married, she says, was unnecessary!

Becky's girls are now thirteen and sixteen. She describes her oldest daughter as "fighting for the underprivileged and anti-establishment." She has had to "break ground," Becky says, being the first one in her class at school to have divorced parents, and the only one in her class to have a mother with a disability. This has made her sensitive to the disadvantaged and critical of teenage popularity and conformism. Her younger daughter, Becky says, is just the opposite. "She wants to be a cheerleader and a peer leader."

As a mother with a disability, Becky has tried to participate as much as she can in her children's school life and activities. When the children were in kindergarten, she participated in the yearly "diversity awareness" programs and though she couldn't help in the gym or take part in school trips, she has made lots of cookies for school events! She feels that both of her girls have taken her disability "as normal" but she also describes their attitude as "bittersweet."

Becky is in a wheelchair now and has Personal Care Assistants daily. She meets other, mostly younger women, with MS in her therapist's office and finds their conversations rewarding. She also notes that she may be the last generation to experience such degenerating MS because now it is diagnosed sooner and drugs have been discovered that are quite effective. Her husband, who suffers some problems from a back injury, has a long commute to work so is away many hours during the day and thus cannot give her a lot of physical help. Becky discovered that in order to get the help she needs under Massachusetts health insurance, she has to work ten hours a week. With the help of friends, she has just started a business called "Mrs. Sprout's Nursery and Landscaping," where she can develop and use her love of plants.

Martha: I felt like a lab specimen, you know

Martha, 26, who has spina bifida, also illustrates the need for more knowledge about the reproductive health of women with disabilities but also the need for more sensitivity training for medical students and residents caring for the women. She describes her experiences in the hospital during her pregnancy when she came in for check-ups and was once admitted to monitor a possible pretoxemia.

Her pregnancy, Martha says, was pretty normal. She had a high risk obstetrician, as suggested by her regular doctor, but she found that the doctor didn't know a great deal about spina bifida and its effect on pregnancy and delivery. "She's not a doctor I would go back to," Martha says. "She didn't really have a bedside manner. She had no personality at all."

"They haven't done a lot of research on pregnant women with disabilities," Martha says. Her doctor gave her one article and Martha tried to research the subject herself, but she didn't find much. She doesn't know if any difficulties she had were due to her disability. "Until enough women who have disabilities have babies, we won't know enough."

About three weeks before her delivery she was kept in the hospital for two days to test for pretoxemia, which turned out negative. It was in this period and also in her check up visits that she experienced the insensitivity of the medical staff.

Medical students and interns continually came into her room to observe her on their rounds. She says, "I felt like a lab specimen, you know."

> They're like, 'Oh there's a girl with a disability and she's pregnant and she's supposed to give birth.' I just got really annoyed. I actually called my mother and said "get these—expletive—medical students out of my room now." [My mother] called the nurses' station and said, 'Look she does not want any medical students touching her in any way, shape or form' and they got the message and stuck a note on the door 'no medical students.

One resident particularly "freaked" her out, Martha says:

> I don't like residents, can you tell? This resident, she says, acted like he knew everything. "I felt like I probably knew more than he did at that point. He gave me a pelvic exam and after he finished, he turned to the nurse—not looking at me—and said, 'That was a very interesting exam' and made a comment about the shape of my uterus. I don't know how I didn't smack the guy. I thought this guy has a medical degree and yet how stupid can he be. That he would actually say that out loud right in front of the patient. This guy just had his hand and his whole fist between my legs and then he says something like that!

Despite her negative experiences with the medical world, Martha's delivery went quite well. She was induced at 37 weeks and given medication but no epidural; the anesthesiologist was not sure what the effect would be on her. Her labor, though painful, was not too long, she says, and her mother and a very attentive nurse stayed with her most of the time and "tried to keep me calm." Her daughter was born naturally without a c-section and she was thrilled when they "wrapped her up and gave her right to me."

Martha also describes the loving support and help she got, as a single parent, from her parents and sister and grandmother. She says, "I had tons of moms around me that I trusted." She had some anxieties and reservations about being a parent at first:

> *I guess at the very beginning I thought 'My god, how am I going to do it! But then I said 'Wait a minute I've said that to myself a million times about other things. I've never not done something that I wanted just because it's difficult. I'm just going to have to find different ways to do things and see what works.*

Martha did find her own way and adaptations in taking care of her child. She recalls some of the best moments of being a mother and being with her baby:

> *Holding her and just hanging out and having her smile. Babies are just so carefree and don't even know what the world's about. You know they are changing and growing and doing different things everyday. It is fun just to see what each day will bring. And it's still that way. They change all the time.*

5. THE POST PARTUM EXPERIENCE

The post partum experience is a defining one for disabled mothers. It is the moment when they have to figure out how they are going to carry, change, feed, dress and bathe their infant despite the limitations of their particular disability. They usually need some support system. Most of the women interviewed had planned how they were going to get support when they returned from the hospital. Talia had excellent help from a doula. Kathy was surrounded with family and friends as well as daily personal assistants. Laura shared care giving with her spouse. For women with disabilities, these initial tests of care giving not only challenge their physical capabilities but also bring home the importance of having the help they need.

However, if, as in Phouvieng's case, no family or friends are available and finances prohibit having aids, the early weeks and months are particularly difficult because, as Phouvieng discovered, there is no help available from state or local social services. She was on her own.

Adaptation and improvisation is particularly important in coping with infant care. For instance, as described by Kathy and others, they make sure there are duplicate supplies in different rooms—or upstairs and downstairs (if that is appropriate); they find adaptive equipment, such as cribs that have sliding sides so you can sit beside them and reach in to lift out the infant; they use equipment creatively, such as strollers or rolling bassinets or wheelchairs, to move the infant from one room to another. Diaper changing is often done on the bed instead of on a changing table so that the mother can sit and be more secure. Bathing a baby can be done by taking a bath in the tub with the baby while the other parent stands by to help. A mother with a weak arm wrapped Velcro around the back of her wheelchair and over the child, securing him on her lap while bottle feeding. And she used baby clothes with zippers instead of snaps, which were difficult for her fingers to fasten.

Even with plans and support systems, these mothers often felt anxiety. As Kathy said, she did not want to be alone the first three weeks and another mother confided that she felt that her husband expected too much of her in coping with infant care. Non-disabled mothers also share this experience of stress as new mothers. In a study of women's post partum experience, Christa Kelleher (2003) writes that partly due to the high cost of hospital stays, the medical world shifted in the second half of the 20th century from a focus after childbirth on the mother to the infant, which has impacted postpartum care. Women have shorter stays in the hospital after the delivery and are sent home and expected to be "independent and self-sufficient mothers." Kelleher concludes that it is time for a greater focus on women's post partum needs (p. 287). Disabled mothers, especially, could use more focus on their needs.

6. THE MOTHERHOOD EXPERIENCE

All of these women agreed that having a child was probably the most important happening in their life. Talia and Molly spoke of being transformed as women by becoming mothers. Talia, echoing Denise, the adoptive mother, spoke of the self-confidence she has gained in herself that she didn't know she had. Phouvieng described the amazing bond she has with her daughters. Another mother says, "I tell my babies that my life was changed the second you were born... nothing I would do after that would be the same."

Anne Finger (1990), in *Past due: A story of disability, pregnancy and birth,* was one of the first to write about the actual experience of pregnancy, birth and postpartum care by a woman with a disability. She captures the transformative nature of becoming a mother as well as its intense physicality for a disabled woman. She writes that her love for her infant "grows from the physical root." She describes the hard work of her experience: "Motherhood is exhaustion and feeling helpless." And about her particular limitation with polio, she writes, "It's the slowness that I notice most. I walk at half the pace most people do (except when I'm tired, then I'm even slower). That means that almost every household chore takes at least twice as long." (p. 177) Despite its challenges, Finger describes becoming a mother as transformative. She writes that motherhood has opened up to her love and empathy for the global world of motherhood:

> *Motherhood is this river of love, a door into the world without clock-time, it is the world cracked open and made new and it is this physical ache, the weariness seeping out from my bones, this dopey haze of love.* (p. 178).

LESSONS TO SHARE

For Mothers with Disabilities

Assume that you CAN have children. You have the freedom to choose.

Consult genetic counseling if you are worried about passing on a genetic condition and want to know your options.

Choose a physician carefully—a high risk obstetrician if possible; one who knows about your particular disability.

Coordinate physicians—gynecologist, neurologist, physiatrist, obstetrician—and put together a team to take you through pregnancy and childbirth.

Do your own research and provide written information to your physician about your particular disability if necessary.

Closely monitor your medical care through pregnancy.

Consult practical guidebooks on pregnancy and childbirth for women with disabilities (see Works Cited)

See that your postpartum support system is in place: adaptations in the household, assistance needed.

Acknowledge that you may feel overwhelmed when you first come home from the hospital. Postpartum depression can be experienced by mothers—able bodied or disabled.

For Physicians and Health Care Professionals

Make your offices accessible to all people with disabilities.

Train medical students, particularly in gynecology and obstetrics, to have some knowledge of different disabilities and to know how each disability affects a woman's reproductive system and her pregnancy and childbirth.

Train medical students, interns and residents, to be sensitive to a disabled woman's privacy. Don't make her feel like a case study when interacting with her.

Be willing to work as a team of physicians and health professionals in caring for the pregnancy and childbirth of a woman with a disability.

For Social Workers

While she is in the hospital, check to see if she needs any practical advice or help in preparations for taking her child home.

Acknowledge possible post partum difficulties—physical or emotional—and remove the pressure of her feeling she has "to do it all."

Chapter Two

Care Giving and Mothers with Disabilities

The Early Years

All mothers feel some anxiety when they realize that the responsibility and care for their wonderful child is primarily theirs. Disabled mothers can feel this more intensely because they are particularly anxious to prove themselves a "good mother," which in our culture usually includes performing the actual physical tasks of child caring. Disabled mothers cannot always do all of these tasks or sometimes any of them. In the following stories women describe their care giving strategies and the changes they make in their environment to fit their needs. They talk about their young children's responses as they develop in their first formative years before school and they particularly highlight ways in which they excel in caring for the psychological and emotional needs of their children. They all confront the issue of dependency on others in caring for their child.

Just about everyone experiences giving and receiving care sometime in their lives, but we seldom think about the complex nature of the relationships involved. Feminists have often discussed the question of care giving from the caregiver's point of view. They argue that since society assumes that care giving is "natural" to women, they are often exploited in this role. Even when they address the issue from the point of view of the disabled woman, feminists have described these mothers as" doubly disadvantaged," thus making them seem like victims—a characterization that disabled mothers wish to avoid at all costs (Watson and McKie, 2002, p.335). In contrast, disability activists, seeing the issue from the care receivers' point of view, emphasize the disempowerment disabled women experience when they receive care. If they are seen exclusively as "care receivers" and dependents, they are often perceived as unfit to be "caregivers" and thus unfit as mothers (Grue and Laerum, 2001, p. 673). They argue that disabled women need to be validated as mothers. Since both feminists and disability activists share the goal of empowering all women, they can agree that care giving must be redefined. It must be seen as interdependent and as a recognition of changing mutual needs that is ongoing (Watson and McKie, 2002, p. 340).

Susan Wendell (1997) in "Toward a Feminist Theory of Disability" argues for a model of reciprocity in care giving. She quotes Barbara Hillyer Davis' s definition of this model: "Reciprocity involves the difficulty of recognizing each others needs, relying on the other, asking and receiving help, delegating responsibility, giving and receiving empathy, respecting boundaries (Davis, 1984, p. 4)." Wendell concludes that all feminists—able-bodied and disabled—have to question our cultural obsession with independence and change social values to recognize the value of depending on others and being depended upon (p. 273). Mothers with disabilities and their caregivers need to experience this reciprocity.

Nancy Mairs (1995), in *Waist High in the World*, shares her understanding of care giving as a mother who feels a frustration with her increasing dependency on others as her physical condition deteriorates from multiple sclerosis. She acknowledges that despite her increasing regret of no longer being the caregiver, "Permitting myself to be taken care of is, in fact, one of the ways I can take care of others (p. 83)." Mairs accepts the fact that she needs help and knows, by accepting it, she is relieving her family's worry about her safety and thus she is still taking care of them.

This notion of reciprocity can be applied to the relationship of a disabled mother and her able bodied child. We'll illustrate this further in Part Four's discussion of able bodied children's family relationships with a disabled mother. In the present chapter, the accounts of mothers with young children show that often the children learn quickly to adjust to a mother or parent's particular disability and circumstances and are instinctively helpful. One mother noted how her toddler very quickly learned how to climb up and sit on her lap in her wheelchair. At two, Kate's daughter "rolled around" in her mother's scooter, sitting on her lap. Cindy spoke of her son, at three, sitting on the floor beside his father's wheelchair. Lorrie said that her daughter, Cynthia, at three, carried her baby sister around and helped to feed her.

Another way in which these mothers with disabilities illustrate the principle of interdependence that shapes their lives is the kind of "shared care giving" they experience with family, spouse, and often other helpers. Sometimes they use PCAs (personal care assistants) for their own physical daily needs. In most states, as part of Medicaid services, they cannot use them to help with the children so they have to pay out of pocket for help with child care tasks that they would ordinarily do themselves. The relationships with assistants can become very intertwined. Organizing and relating to helpers takes skill and tact. Chris, whose story was included in Part One, made sure that the friends and helpers understood that they should not try to be a substitute mother but rather help *her* to carry out the mothering tasks for her infant twins.

The women interviewed here have varying degrees of physical limitations and therefore different challenges in balancing their needs, but all of them felt pressure to prove themselves to be "good mothers." Those who needed a lot of care particularly wrestled with the issue of "shared care giving."

SHARED CARE GIVING

"A parent is still parenting and providing care for a child when others help in providing this care." (Mullin 2005, p. 183)

Several different patterns emerged about shared care giving in the women interviewed in this chapter. One was co-parenting with a spouse who was able-bodied, another was co-parenting with a spouse who was also disabled and another was a single parent, in this case, a disabled mother who, after a divorce, was parenting alone. Because of the varying degrees of physical limitations, the amount of outside/paid help needed varied, from extensive use of personal care assistants—sometimes who lived in—to regular or occasional use of home help.

Kate, who became a single mom, needs live-in personal care assistants and Cindy, who co-parents, uses daily PCAs who don't live in. The two women illustrate different challenges in adapting to their physical limitations as mothers. They negotiate and resolve their conflicting needs of receiving and giving care.

Kate: I think the biggest struggle for us with my disability has been that we have needed people in the house to help us physically on a regular basis since my daughter was five years old

Kate, born in 1951, was diagnosed with multiple sclerosis in 1981. Her daughter, Sarah, was born in 1985. Kate had symptoms of MS before her pregnancy—numbness in one hand and leg—but she had no diagnosis after going to three different neurologists and many tests. "You can't really give a definitive diagnosis of MS until you watch it for a while," she says. Finally, she found "my good doctor," who knew right away and said, of all the tests, "That's a shame, they put you through all that."

Kate's pregnancy and delivery, however, went very well. She had a very supportive team—an obstetrician and a neurologist—and a successful natural delivery. "The birth was really quite a victory for me, and even for my husband," Kate says.

After the birth, the MS "did get markedly worse," Kate adds. She was already having some difficulty in walking and had gotten a scooter for long walks, but now she had more problems. "I used to be able to stand up from the bed and now I couldn't easily stand up any more." "There can be a lot of losses with MS, a lot of grieving to go with it," Kate reflects.

Like many disabled mothers, Kate changed her environment to fit her needs in caring for her daughter. "With the help of family, including my husband, and other relatives, I did feel pretty capable physically for the first year and a half," Kate says, "I adapted." Although her bedroom was on the second floor, Kate arranged the downstairs so she could stay there all day. She brought down a bassinette and set up a changing area around the couch. She was able to transfer Sarah back and forth in her scooter and until she got a stair chair, she hired a neighborhood teenager to come and carry Sarah upstairs at night. The formula bottles were kept in a cooler on the second floor and warmed in hot running water for night feedings. She got an adapted van with hand controls so she was able to drive and get her daughter into the car seat.

Sarah was walking at nine months so the question of safety and discipline came up quickly. Kate was in her scooter so "when she was walking inside, I felt assured that I could reach her if necessary." But, she continues, "When she was outside, I didn't feel we were totally secure." When Sarah was a toddler, Kate tried using a harness when they went to the park together. "This never felt really right for Sarah, who was a great explorer from the age of fourteen months," Kate says. "I felt she should be able to run around, so I had to try other methods to keep her safe." Once when Sarah was four, Kate even decided to get into her van and pretend to drive away until Sarah ran to get into the car. "My lovely daughter was a little defiant one," she says smiling, "and I think in some ways, that was just her strong independent personality. She was testing the limits of Mommy and seeing what Mommy could deal with. To this day we have a relationship of humor and contentiousness!"

Other issues of discipline came up as well. For instance, in Sarah's relationships with other children, she had to learn how to share. If she grabbed a toy from another child in the park, Kate was not able to physically intervene, but she tried to talk to Sarah before they went out, explaining what was not acceptable and that if she misbehaved, she and Mommy would have to go home. And then she would have to follow up and leave if an incident occurred. "I do feel testing is just part of her personality" Kate says, but "I think it's been exacerbated by my disability." And, she laughs, "Also, I'm just a soft touch. I was a bit too nice as a teacher way before I had MS!"

With her van, Kate was able to get out and do a lot with Sarah. They went swimming together at the YMCA and enjoyed outings to museums and nature centers with other friends and their children. The playgroup was more than willing to meet at her house so that Sarah could enjoy friendships before she went to nursery school

Kate: When it came time for us to say goodbye and put Sarah back in my lap, she reached for Susan

Kate remembers that one of the most painful parts of being restricted to her scooter was when her daughter would reach for other grownups to pick her up. She remembers going to a holiday dinner and having her cousin, Susan, carry Sarah around with her and mingle among the guests. She says, "I couldn't carry her and when it came time for us to say goodbye and put Sarah back in my lap, she cried and reached for Susan. And that was very hard. It broke my heart. But, I could really, really understand what she was feeling."

Despite her occasionally turning to other grown ups, Sarah was very attached to her mother in her first three or four years. Kate says, "I think almost overly attached. When she started nursery school, her father, who was still with them, had to take her the first few days because she wouldn't get off my lap in the scooter. Her father could take her by the hand and walk her in and she could hold onto his leg but then he was free to leave."

Kate feels Sarah's separation issues and insecurities had something to do with her mother's disability. Kate recalls that at about four, Sarah, like many children, began to think about death and worried that her mother might not always be with her. Once when Kate was sitting with Sarah as she got ready to go to sleep, her daughter asked her if she was going to die from her disability. Kate reassured her, but it was hard for her to articulate because she did not know the limits of her progressive disease and if she would have many years with her daughter. She tried to explain that she might get a little less strong, but that there were all kinds of things to help her and that she was going to be around for a long, long time. Kate says, "She accepted that. Then came the question, 'Why can't I have a sister?' And I felt sad for her. I really wanted her to have a sibling."

Having another child was out of the question because Kate's energy was diminishing and her marriage was under stress. "I want to have all my energy for you," she said to her daughter. Eight years later, she separated from her husband, Peter. They were divorced in 1998.

I asked her if she thought her disability played a part in that. She said, "Absolutely, although we'll never really know if we would have divorced anyhow, because of personality differences. But it just became really pronounced dealing with a chronic illness and how we coped with that. We became so at odds with each other." She continued:

> I think had he been the type of person who was more able to rise above the losses that come with a progressive disability, we might have been able to stay

*together longer. He was a really good person, but his depression about my
disability made him negative and we didn't want to see our daughter raised
around that much unhappiness.*

Kate: She [Sarah] had to deal with personalities of many other people

Kate had personal care assistants in the home before her divorce and she
considers her need to have other people living with them a major difficulty
for her daughter and a challenge for herself in managing conflicting needs.
She needed help in the mornings in dressing and getting downstairs and
doing daily tasks so her daughter would have to wait sometimes while her
mother's needs were taken care of. Sarah's father had to leave for work very
early, so Sarah had to learn to be both patient and independent at a very
young age.

"But beyond that," says Kate, "she had to deal with the personalities of
others. And they might be there for six months or a year and Sarah would get
attached to them and then they would leave. One lady from South Africa
stayed for four years and really became part of the family. Those were some
of our best years."

But other experiences were painful for everyone. Another assistant to
whom Sarah became attached was there the day, Peter, Sarah's father, moved
out. Kate remembers:

> *Of all days, that night all the lights went off in the house at about six or seven
> and Sarah ran to the helper in sobs and not to me. I understand Sarah was
> angry and frightened about the separation and about being left with a disabled
> Mom. But inside I was in tears myself. Ironically, that particular assistant
> stayed for three years but then stole Sarah's laptop when she left.*

More recently Kate began hiring some college students as assistants. They
stayed about six months or a year. She also reaches out to other people and
invites them to come and live in her house, like a nephew and his girl friend,
who are staying with her now. Someone once pointed out, "It's kind of like a
halfway house," laughs Kate.

Kate: She's [Sarah] definitely a survivor, but she's been angry

I asked Kate if she felt that her daughter experienced anger about having to
be independent because her mother had a disability. She said, yes, for sure.
"She's definitely a survivor, but she's been angry. And I think I validated her
anger a lot."

She remembers that when she used crutches in the early years when Sarah
was four, her daughter said, "I hate those crutches. Mom, you don't need

them." And I said, "You know what? They help Mom get around. But I sure wish I didn't need them."

She also recalls that after talking to a third grade class with Sarah about what it was like to live with a disability, one of the children asked Sarah if she gets mad about her mother's disability and Sarah replied, "Yes I do get mad. I punch the pillow and yell."

But Kate adds, "She's really a feisty, independent, bright and funny kid." She laughs, "She has always been a wise ass, a lot of back talk. It's been hard sometimes."

Sarah has grown up now and is twenty-two. She went to high school and then on to college, majoring in business. She's living at home this year with a current roommate and working as an office manager.

Kate says, "She's always been business oriented. She loved counting her change…and then she would smile. It was hysterical. Very, very organized. I kid her to this day."

But, Kate adds, "She can still be quick to anger, but now, instead of griping about the situation, she is talking with me when I say, "You know, you seem angry. Let me know what you are thinking."

I asked Kate what her daughter is angry about. She responded:

> Sarah feels that her mother is constantly unreliable. And that is absolutely true. It's the nature of the situation. But we continue to hash things out and look at what is the stress of the disability and what are my shortcomings that I have to own up to. Being disabled is not an excuse for bad behavior. At times it seems as if we've been in two separate places. But it also feels good to have the time living together to work it out.

Sarah has also expressed concern about her mother's increasing physical needs and about managing her staff of workers. Kate says, "She's a straight shooter and said, 'Mom, you have to start compartmentalizing your needs so that people have assigned duties around the house.' And I just looked at her and smiled, "You are such a business major, and so smart. And I said, thanks. Thanks for your advice."

About her daughter, Kate concludes, "She gives me the same amount of grief she would give any mother, which is in a way a compliment!"

Kate has dealt with many challenges in her life—her deteriorating physical condition that brings conflicts to her as a mother and a wife and her financial and special medical needs. Her reaction is to reach out to others both in her private life and more publicly as an advocate for promoting the understanding of disability. She has worked in programs at a medical school and a public school. She serves on a committee to improve wages and benefits for PCAs "thereby stabilizing the lives of the people in need of their services," she says.

Early on in the interview Kate expressed concern and sympathy for the younger men and women she has met in MS support groups. She sees them struggle, as she did, with the changes in their lives and their desire to stay "normal."

"There are losses to reckon with," she says, "after every new challenge." But continuing to reflect on her own experience. Kate says, "At this point, I actually feel on an even keel. At this point I've got about everything I need. At last I feel I can sit back a little. I feel retired! It's a bit like being retired!"

Cindy: I am the mother. I am in charge

Cindy, already mentioned in Part One, is a spinal cord quadriplegic. Her impairments are severe but remain relatively stable. She parents their son, Tanner, with her husband, Ted, who also has a spinal cord injury. Cindy's story shows us a different challenge and strategy of negotiating care giving and care receiving.

Cindy, born in 1958, became a quadriplegic after an automobile accident when she was eighteen. Needing considerable physical care since her injury, she has fought successfully for independence. About her maternal role, she says, "I am the mother. I am in charge."

I met Cindy in her office at Mass Rehab where she is a Rehabilitation Counselor. She met me at the door in her power wheelchair and we talked at her desk about her experience of having a child and raising him with her husband. She spoke of balancing her work, her physical needs, and bringing up a "normal kid."

Cindy's spinal cord injury caused extensive paralysis. She has some use of her arms and upper body with the help of splints. Her mother was a loving caregiver but, Cindy, after a long rehabilitation, was anxious for more independence. She had been popular socially in high school and continued to have boy friends. But, she says, "I did all the breaking up!" She finally moved in with a boy friend, but it turned out that he, like her mother, wanted to be a "caregiver." She says, "It ruined the relationship." With the help of personal care assistants, Cindy was able to get her own apartment and achieved the independence she sought.

Cindy attended Mount Wachusett Community College and Assumption College where she is working toward an M.A. in Social Rehabilitation Counseling. Her first job was in skills training and peer counseling for those in transition to independent living. She has been with Mass Rehab since then and drives an adapted van to work every day.

When Cindy met Ted, they became engaged after four months. After they'd been married and began to think about having a child, they met disbelief and astonishment from their doctors, but they persisted, assisted by the fact that Cindy's father-in-law was an important obstetrician at her doctor's hospital. She and her husband attended a fertility clinic for insemination for three months and when she became pregnant, a comprehensive team of medical professionals was put together to guide her through the pregnancy and delivery. An ABC documentary, "Amazing Families" chronicles in a two-part series, Cindy's experience. Part One includes the preparations and consultations of the medical team, the three hospitalizations during her pregnancy, her delivery and return home and their first months with their son. The second part shows the raising of Tanner, their son, an active happy kid of eight.

Cindy has always had personal care assistants; in addition, a life long friend comes to help her get up and prepare for work every morning. In the documentary we get an idea of the small but ingenious strategies that can help someone with limited mobility. Cindy uses a table top where she can stretch out while her attendant helps to arrange and straighten her clothes. Cindy does her hair and make up herself. She has had a number of other attendants. "Wonderful girls," she says, "like an extended family."

Ted, her husband, who is more functional, was able to lift Tanner as an infant from his crib and to the changing table and other places, using his wheel chair. Cindy says Tanner was a good baby and slept though the night. She also added that, as a toddler, he used to sit by his father at the foot of his wheelchair. Ted, who is a teacher, changed jobs when Tanner began school so that he could be home when his son arrived on the bus. He also plays catch with Tanner and is an assistant coach from his wheelchair for his son's basketball team.

Cindy: I run the show

"I run the show," says Cindy. She has never felt that she cannot fulfill her role as a mother. She buys Tanner's clothes and helps him decide what to wear and oversees his hygiene, his homework, among other things, and organizes his activities. She admits she may overcompensate a bit because of her fear of other people judging her as not a "good enough" mother, but she is relieved to see that Tanner is a regular kid and has friends at school and friends in the neighborhood. She has never expected him to do any personal care for her or Ted, but he does normal chores that any child might do.

Tanner is very aware of his parents' physical limitations, but, Cindy feels, he is not embarrassed or angered by them. He speaks of having "cool parents." Cindy laughs and wonders if that is because of the nifty adaptive van they have. In the second part of the documentary film, there is a family photo of Cindy and Ted side by side in their wheelchairs and Tanner standing at the top of his mother's wheel chair on which he has climbed. A spectator, who was watching the film, said, "He sees his mother's chair not as a wheelchair but as a jungle gym." That is what his parents have hoped to achieve.

Cindy and Ted worked out a successful plan of shared responsibilities. They are fortunate to have adequate financial means and abundant support from family and friends. They have also put enormous thought and energy into working together as a family and Cindy has shown, ever since her injury, a determined sense of independence and self assurance though she still admits she is conscious of trying to prove herself as a mother.

Cindy and Ted together make a good team in caring for and raising their son. Perhaps because they both have disabilities they can understand each other's needs. But there is no magic formula for ideal parenting, let alone the kind of shared parenting that exists when one or both parents have a disability. These stories suggest that, like most parents, circumstances and personalities complicate teamwork. A mother with a disability whose husband is able-bodied has her own story to tell.

Lorrie: He [her husband] is much more involved than a lot of fathers, but he is still not a mom

Lorrie has cerebral palsy and Ed, her husband, is able bodied. They work as a team but Lorrie says they have had their differences.

Speaking about sharing the care of their second child, Lorrie, who is 36, says, "I think Ed and I have both been surprised by the level of fighting that goes on between us. We've actually joked about if we had a third child, we would probably get a divorce. We are older and more set in our ways, more selfish."

On the other hand, thinking back on their life together, she says, "Ours is a marriage that is very equitable. He [my husband] knew that he was going to have to pony up 50% because of my disability. We have our little squabbles and arguments about what his 50% entails. I think a lot of that is just him being a man. He is much more involved than a lot of fathers, but he is still not a mom."

Lorrie is refreshingly frank about her experience of motherhood. Talking about her first months of taking care of her infant daughter, Cynthia, she says, "I don't enjoy being a baby momma. I feel bad about it because society wants every mom to just love and adore her baby." She also says about her two girls, 6 and 13 months, "I can't imagine my life without them now."

But, she says, it was her husband who really wanted to have children. "I truly enjoy kids and I taught at Sunday school for years but I could just take them or leave them." After they had been married for four years, they decided to try to get pregnant. "My husband is very family oriented and I'm family oriented and so it made sense." She asked her obstetrician if her disability could cause a problem and he said no, so they went ahead and found that Lorrie was pregnant almost immediately.

Both families were thrilled when they heard of Lorrie's pregnancy, particularly her husband's who had disapproved of the marriage, partly because Lorrie is not Catholic, but mostly, Lorrie thinks, because of her disability. "In their eyes, she says, "he was going to have to take care of me," but the family was reassured and overjoyed at the news of an expected grandchild.

Lorrie: Look, I need a little more help

Lorrie has never felt particularly disabled, though she has some weakness in one hand and one foot. Her family, she says, "treated me like I could do anything." Being pregnant and having the children has made Lorrie more aware of her disability. She admits that sometimes she wishes that "she was treated a little more special," particularly with the pregnancy and birth of Emily, their second child. At 36, she found that her body had changed and could not handle the stress as easily. She ended up with a stress fracture in her right foot but everyone, including her husband, minimized her condition. She describes her conflicting feelings about the pregnancy and her husband's attitude:

> *I had to fight a lot more with my husband, to say 'Look, I'm not normal.' I didn't want to have to say it out loud, but, you know, it was hard to say 'Look, I need a little more help here.' His family is not used to me asking him for help. He also had a problem with the fact that I was not quite as gung ho about the second child—though now I can't imagine not having her here. It completes the family—But he likes to think only of the positives—another little baby to love and to hug—and I was thinking 'another baby I'd have to carry around for another nine months.'*

"I'm not a very happy good pregnant person," says Lorrie. She had pre-term labor with Cynthia and "I was completely terrified. "She gained forty pounds and says, "I think once I got to the ninth month, I was just ready to be done with it."

After the ankle fracture in the second pregnancy, the doctor put her in a walking cast for six weeks. When she called Ed he asked if she was sure that was what the doctor wanted her to do. She was angry. What she really wanted from him was validation that this was the right treatment.

> *"I have a little bit of drama queen in me," she laughed. "I wanted him to tell me that this was the best decision. He is one of those people who is just 'you do what you need to do.' She adds, "There are times when I need someone to sort of kick me in the butt and say 'you really need to do this!'"*

Lorrie had natural births for both children. She was in the hospital for six days after Cynthia's birth because of a retained placenta, which meant blood transfusions and a D&E [dilation and evacuation] on Mother's Day and so she didn't even go to the nursery until the fifth day. Her husband was the one who did the initial bonding with Cynthia. With Emily, the birth was easy and she had the baby with her by herself more. She remembers thinking, "So this is what it's like not feeling special about just giving birth. You have in the back of your mind the other kid. I talked to her [Cynthia] every day on the phone."

I asked Lorrie if anyone in the hospital—a social worker, for instance—talked to her about how she would take care of the baby. She says, "No. I guess I wished that someone had come in and said 'So, you have a disability, do you know how to change a diaper?' I had never changed a diaper in my life. I watched the video on the baby care channel that they pipe in and that was pretty much it."

Lorrie feels initially she was very naïve managing the realities of motherhood. She thought nursing would be a breeze but found, because of the weakness of one hand, she couldn't manage holding the baby and her breast to the baby at the same time. She explains with amusement: "After we got the five pillows laid around me and my husband is holding my boob just so, I'm thinking 'this is absolutely crazy. Ed has to go to work. So, ultimately we decided to pump and bottle feed and that worked fine!"

For about six weeks Lorrie had help from her mom and dad and her in-laws, but then she was on her own. She didn't have any nurses or attendants. And she didn't expect it to be so difficult. She realizes that part of the problem is that she hasn't thought about her disability much. She remembers: "I'm probably guilty of not really thinking of myself as having a disability and then I think 'Oh shit! I do have a disability and that's why this is harder for me and I have to give myself a break. I have to say 'that makes sense now.'"

"The first day you are by yourself, you really don't want to be by yourself," she says. "With Cynthia it was all new and I remember being very proud of myself for changing a diaper. But it just takes a long time for me to get a child ready in the morning. I've watched my husband do it and I think to myself 'that's what it's like!'"

She recalls that Cynthia was particularly hard to get diapered because she kept turning over on the changing table. "We have gotten into knock down fights. I have a temper. She has a temper. When I talk to other people about it, I don't think they quite get how difficult it is to be struggling with a child and only have one hand. It's hard to know that you need to do something for your child and not be able physically to do it."

Besides realizing and accepting the fact of her physical limitations in a new way, Lorrie also finds that she and her husband have developed different methods of caring for the children, though they share the tasks and often work separately, each taking a child. Ed likes to change and dress Emily standing up, but Lorrie, of course, can't manage that and doesn't want Emily to expect it.

Mostly, Lorrie says, they do the caring for each child in tandem. She'll take one child and he'll take the other. He typically takes Cynthia to the birthday parties while she stays home with Emily. They try to make sure that each girl has special time with each parent.

"I have been taking Cynthia to the grocery store a little bit more or just taking her out. In part because now she can get in and out of the car by herself." She finds that she can't include Emily very easily, but she can take her to and from day care and to friends' houses to visit. She adds "Cynthia is wonderful with her baby sister. She will carry her around, will feed her, will comfort her. She enjoys that."

Lorrie describes the routine of taking care of small children as "going in waves." "It will be real easy for a long time," she says, "and then all of a sudden it completely falls apart. And you go, 'Who is this child?'"

She also finds that she and her husband also "step up to the plate" more or less periodically, one doing more while the other does less.

Lorrie feels strongly about wanting to be a successful mother. She says, "Sometimes I am very upset that I'm not going to be as successful as other moms who have two good hands, or who can do things better. I don't really cook. I have always found cooking hard—cutting things up, dumping out a pot. I don't feel I need to do it but I sort of wonder if Cynthia is missing something, not learning how to cook."

On the other hand, Lorrie feels Cynthia, and eventually Emily, too, is learning other important things. "She has learned a lot about disability and a lot about diversity and tolerance and understanding. We talk about "my little hand" and "my little foot" and that's how she understands and it's just normal for her."

She is sometimes amazed when she realizes her children will do things she will never be able to do. They will wear high heel shoes! They will have good balance. She had a revelation when she realized Cynthia was going down stairs without holding on to the railing. "I had an epiphany that she doesn't necessarily need to hold on. She doesn't need to be as careful as I am!"

Thinking about her goals as a mother, Lorrie says:

> I want to nurture and help Cynthia and Emily to grow into independent and strong women, I want both daughters to feel that they can do anything they want to do, that's how I was raised. I truly believe it's my job to phase myself out of a job. I'm looking forward to them growing up and to what they are going to be like.

When asked what would be most helpful to her as a mom with a disability, Lorrie reflected a bit and said:

> *I don't know, I want to say something about car seat construction, that you have to have two hands to get the car seat in and out of the car or to drop the handle down to get the baby out of the seat. I wish there were more gadgets designed for me specifically with my disability—being left handed—with one hand that does not have much range of motion or dexterity. I've gone to some of the parenting workshops and I have found I am not disabled enough for a lot of stuff to be useful. There's probably a group of us that are high functioning but just a little assistance would make a lot of difference.*

Following up on these suggestions, Lorrie warns other women with disabilities that they are a "different shade" when they become a mother. She says, "I know for me, before I had kids, if I couldn't do something, it wasn't that big a deal. It wasn't affecting anyone else. With children, if you can't do something or you can't do it with ease, it is really, really hard."

But, she insists you need to give yourself a break. "All moms beat themselves up too much. Society talks about 'Oh, everyone wants to be a mom. Just look at Angelina Jolie, carting off to Africa.' I'm thinking where is the diaper bag? We've been brainwashed into thinking it's so easy. It's hard for any mom, but it's harder for a mom with a disability."

Lorrie gives us another configuration of shared care giving. Her team includes a husband who is able bodied, which is obviously a big advantage. But as she explains, it doesn't mean there are no tensions and adjustments to make with each other. And she still feels that as a "mom" she has the major care giving role. She often feels her physical limitations and realizes she was less aware of them before she became a mother.

Joan: I was very much concerned about fulfilling the role…as a wife and mother

Joan, born in 1932, had polio at twelve. She also has an able bodied husband. He is a research professor and they lived in a college town, bringing up children in the fifties. At that time a wife and mother traditionally stayed home and took care of the children and did the housekeeping. Despite her disability, Joan was able to follow that model of mothering. She says, "I was very much concerned about fulfilling the role, doing what I should be able to do as a wife and mother."

Joan's polio primarily affected one leg and after five operations as a teenager, she was able to stand up alone with one leg brace and crutches and have considerable mobility. "I had lots of vitality and endurance," she says, "and could walk around freely and walk a distance of a mile or more if needed." She says that as a wife and mother she approached adapting to her disability "the same way I always have done ever since I had polio, which was to figure out how I could do it. I can usually work out something," she concludes.

Joan was married in the mid fifties after graduating from the University of Massachusetts where she majored in Biology. She says, "This was before the pill came out and planning and making decisions about having children wasn't quite as easy as it is now a days. The average number of children people had was three or four and I was the eldest of a family of four children so that seemed perfectly natural to me." Joan has four children, born in 1956, '57, '60 and '63. Three boys and one girl and now, two granddaughters.

Because of her disability and the operations in her teenage years, Joan says she had very little experience with little children and her husband, an only son, had no experience. However, she did have ideas about natural childbirth and had read a book, *Natural Childbirth* by Grantly Dick-Read, now considered the father of the natural childbirth movement but much criticized at the time. As a biology major, Joan says, "To me pregnancy and childbirth and breastfeeding were just completing the natural cycle, and I like that." She also felt she had been taught after her orthopedic operations how to relax to help avoid pain.

Joan had natural childbirths for all of her children. Although she had gone to an obstetrician for the first birth, her next two were with her primary care physician, who did deliveries and lived a few miles away. For her fourth child she had a new doctor who sent her to a neurologist. Joan says, "None of the doctors had any knowledge of orthopedic management of pregnancy." Fortunately, she didn't need special care.

Her second child was born at home, though that was not planned and she went to the hospital immediately afterwards with the doctor and the baby. She vividly recalls the scene at her second son's birth. When at one a.m. she woke up and suspected that her baby was coming quickly, she called her doctor and told him "this baby is going to be born here." The doctor came.

> He asked for newspaper and soap and I sent my husband for a new bar of soap and he said he didn't know where it was. But anyway it worked out fine. My mother was there to take care of the other child and when the baby was born the doctor had him in a hand towel looped; he was holding his hands up on either corner and had the baby suspended in a hammock sort of thing, if you get the picture and he said, 'What shall I do with this?' and my mother said, 'I will take him' and so she held him. But anyway that worked out well.

Joan's most frequent comment in her interview is "so that worked out well." In fact, at one point she laughs, saying I seem to be saying that a lot. The account of how she cared for four small children—she focuses on that primarily—is a testament to the extraordinarily careful and inventive ways she managed to do "everything that was necessary" on her own without any assistance from anyone. Her husband was, of course, supportive of the family and took up certain tasks that she could not do or that were more appropriate for a husband at the time, such as building a shelf or a platform.

Joan thoroughly details her adaptations in caring for her infants and toddler children. She breastfed all four children which, she says "made a big difference to me in terms of convenience because you can do it anywhere and anytime and the baby doesn't have time to get terribly worked up crying for a bottle." She also notes that she was ahead of her time because only 50% or less of mothers chose breast feeding in those days.

For night feedings, Joan says, "I didn't even have to get out of bed." She kept the baby right beside her in a carriage which she used instead of a crib for the first three months. Joan was definitely in charge of her infants. She says, if she woke up and her child was crying, "I was able to get out of bed fast and navigate on all fours without my brace," prompting her visiting mother in-law to comment, "I don't know how you get there so fast."

During the day she used the carriage to move the baby around the apartment. The couch was the center of activity with a pile of cloth diapers nearby. Their large wooden playpen was in front of the couch where the children played while she was vacuuming or cooking or doing other chores. Her kitchen was galley style, where she could stand in one place and move dishes along the counter and even into the other room. They bought a small portable washing machine that had a hose that drained into the sink. Her husband would often take the clothes to the dryers in the apartment laundry room but Joan also used racks in the bathtub or hall to dry some of the clothes. They had moved from a tiny studio apartment where the first baby was born to a small but adequate two bedroom apartment owned by the university where they stayed until they built and moved to their own house where they could custom design some special conveniences.

Joan: I was still self conscious about my housekeeping shortcomings

Joan admits that she was not good at designating duties. "Temperamentally, I was not one who was at all accustomed to delegating. My mother hadn't either and I just didn't know how to do that or think it was necessary until much later when it was too late." Although she did expect the children to clean their rooms and keep them presentable, she felt it was her role to take care of the house and do the cooking and take care of the children. Though she confesses "I was self conscious about my housekeeping shortcomings."

Joan was actually quite housebound and alone when her four children were young, but she doesn't complain or see her life then negatively. Many able bodied mothers with small children living in the suburbs in the fifties and sixties did complain about their isolation. Their discontent and its causes were described by Betty Freidan in her groundbreaking book, *The Feminist Mystique* (1963), often claimed as starting the second wave of feminism in America.

Joan's account of motherhood does not reflect Freidan's feminist consciousness. Perhaps her goal and success in accomplishing by herself "everything that was necessary" despite her disability was a personal triumph that was fulfilling. Her recollections are happy ones. She remembers the fun her children had on tricycles outside at the apartment complex and when they were even younger, on small scooters in the apartment. And in their own house she remembers looking out of her kitchen window to see the boys playing with friends in their large wooden sandbox, "building roads and using trucks." Although she didn't go out with her children at Halloween—most parents didn't go because it was considered safe for the children then—she made their Halloween costumes.

As a family they didn't go out much in public. "We didn't have the money to go around or to go to restaurants. And people didn't go to restaurants frequently the way they do now. It was not part of my pattern and I usually had a baby in the family that I would be taking care of at home and I really didn't mind." About once a year they would go on a family trip in the station wagon with the children lying down or playing on a plywood platform that her husband built for the back of the car. There were, of course, no car seats available or required.

Joan: That meant a lot to me and I still love to drive

Although Joan doesn't depict her life as confined or constrained when she was on her own taking care of four small children, she does note a moment in her life when she felt truly independent. That was when she learned to drive a car. She was not able to drive until hand controls and automatic transmissions were available and they did not get a car with that equipment until 1969, when her youngest child was six. She says, "That was the last thing I couldn't do which kept me from complete independence!" She continues, "Oh boy, did it feel good! I could explore our neighborhood that I was curious about without having to explain why. That meant a lot to me and I still love to drive."

Joan is consistently confident that there is very little difference in the way she cared for her children compared to able bodied mothers. She says, "I think there is hardly any difference at all. I just had my own ways of doing things but I was able to do everything that mothers ordinarily have to do, except to carry the baby from one place to another." She does not, in fact, acknowledge that her disability affected her role as a wife and mother and her detailed descriptions of the tasks she carried out could be those of an able bodied woman who is meticulous in planning and carrying out her duties.

Except that in Joan's case, she is doing everything with one weak leg in a brace and she is walking with crutches. For her, it is a matter of mind over matter and her goal is to perform all of the usual roles and tasks that mothers do.

Looking at the stories of these four women—Kate, Cindy, Lorrie and Joan, we see that "taking care" gets defined differently depending on the kind of physical limitation the mother has, the care that she needs and that is available, as well as the cultural moment when she was raising young children and, of course, her own personality.

Kate and Cindy particularly had to negotiate being both care receiver and caregiver. They maintained their independence within the bounds of their dependency. Kate, whose progressive MS forced her to periodically change the amount of care she needed, had to negotiate the relationship between changing personal care assistants and her daughter's readjustments to someone new. She developed a relaxed inclusive life style. Cindy was fortunate in having an assistant who was a friend and became permanent in the family life. She also had the stability of a co-parent.

Taking care for these women with disabilities can involve very physical tasks. It can also provide emotional and psychological care and mentoring. Kate, Cindy, and Lorrie clearly defined their roles not only as managers but also as mentors. They encouraged independence but also the commitment to supporting and reaching out to others. They are self-confident and inventive but clearly aware of the difficulties in being a disabled mother. Joan, who protested she faced very few difficulties, nevertheless described in detail the ways in which she actually worked around physical limitations.

For these women, care giving involves others: personal care attendants, helpers, family and friends and spouses, even for Joan who speaks of her "nuclear family." More than most mothers, these women must develop skills in shared care giving. Meg Kocher, a disabled mother, writes, "Our disabilities have forced us to discuss difficult issues of co-parenting and discipline that other parents may not be required to negotiate" (132)

Tammy: It is not if you will be a mother, but how

Tammy tells us another story about caring for her children but also about her reflections on being a mother with a disability. Born in 1970 with cerebral palsy, she is married to Rachid, who had polio. They have two young daughters. Tammy's story shares a conviction with the four women's stories above: they don't doubt their ability to be a mother, but they know they will have to figure out *how* to do it. Tammy says, "It is not *if* you will be a mother, but *how*."

I met and interviewed Tammy at the Women's Studies Research Center at Brandeis University. She drove there in her van and brought her daughters, two year old Gracie and six month old Lilly. Her wheelchair had been fitted with an ingenious device, engineered by her brother-in-law, that had a small baby seat attached to the chair that could swing in and out. She could bring Lily to her lap to sit or nurse, or push her out to sit beside her while she was speaking or otherwise occupied. Gracie kept busy with books and toys or became engaged with my intern, Avi, who took part in the interview.

I asked Tammy if she would like to tell her story in her own words and she said yes, enthusiastically. Here is her story.

JUST KEEP WALKING THROUGH THE DOOR BY TAMMY RAYESS

My name is Tammy. I was born in 1970 to teenage parents, young and in love, married out of high school and very determined to make it even though the odds were against them. Their strong work ethic and core values would serve me well for the challenges ahead. My father was deployed in the army so my grandfather, gramps, as I called him, took my mom to the hospital when she unexpectedly went into labor. My mom, never a complainer and always thinking of others, sent gramps home. She thought that she would just be examined and would call him when it was time to come home, having no idea what she was about to go through. In the early hours of the morning, birth was imminent. There was no known cause for the start of labor. My mom found herself frightened by an unfamiliar experience and in the hands of a cold, insensitive doctor. I was born nine weeks premature; two pounds, eleven ounces. She could only glance at me as she heard the doctor saying, "It will be touch and go for the next seventy-two hours," as he walked out of the room. Fortunately, such carelessness and inattentiveness is no longer a part of the birth experience.

My parenting journey began very differently. It really took hold in 1982 at the age of twelve when I first read the book *A Child Is Born* by Lennart Nilsson. Of course, I had little girl fascination with pregnancy, but at that moment, in the library of my junior high school, I truly understood the miracle of life that would be growing inside me someday. It never really occurred to me that I should think twice about this pursuit because I have cerebral palsy. In fact, turning away from this goal was never an option simply because it might be challenging: it was my job to figure out how to overcome obstacles. In other words, cerebral palsy does not define me or determine what I will or will not attempt in life. I often do not even include it in the list of descriptors I give for myself. Many people thought my parents were cruel for not making some things easier for me, but I disagree. They were by my side every step of the way and by giving me this determination, they gave me a life.

Time moved on as it always does. I made my way though school and two degrees in Occupational Therapy. Achieving these milestones was completely normal for me. However, I became aware that this is not the norm for every disabled person. I realized I am in a position of educating others about living a functional life with a disability. I try to do this by example, by answering questions and by encouraging inclusion and acceptance of people with varying abilities.

I met my husband, Rachid, in 1995 when I moved to North Carolina to complete my clinical fieldwork. Rachid was 23 when we met. I fell in love with his gorgeous smile immediately and soon found out that he is a brilliant engineer. He is also a person with a disability. He contracted polio in 1974 at the age of one. His family tells me that conceptualization, determination and design abilities have been his strong points from a very young age. Despite his problem solving abilities, Rachid told me he did not want to have children. Since there were many unknowns, he wanted all the answers to be in place to make sure we could do the best job. He wanted me to tell him exactly how we were going to overcome every obstacle that we might encounter and I couldn't. No parent has all the answers; able bodied or not. Don't let it scare you. A family will provide the most rewarding and challenging growth experiences of your life. In fact, not knowing all the answers is part of the wonder of the journey. Learning and growing together as a family is important.

Rachid and I dated for seven years before we married. We came to a consensus on children. Since we dated for an extended period of time, we planned on starting a family right away. I knew that there were no contraindications in my particular situation for pregnancy and delivery. I planned on a natural pregnancy and birth experience with no expectation of problems. However, I did want to make sure I had an OB/GYN who had cared for patients with disabilities before. Specifically, I wanted to make sure that my doctor was not likely to rush to cesarean unnecessarily. Fortunately, I have a tendency to do extensive research. I started to interview doctors a year before our wedding day. It took seven months and a high risk OB to meet those qualifications. Within 1 month of our marriage, I was pregnant.

I remember one surprising conversation with my mom in which I brought up that we were planning to start a family soon. Much to my surprise, she paused. For a moment, I panicked not knowing how to take it if she resisted but she said only "you know, you will have to be much more domestic and prepare food every day." She was not doubting my ability to take care or to parent but to do that which I had resisted forever—cooking. That conversation was a turning point for me. I had always been very career oriented. Never accepting the traditional roles for a woman up to that point, I found myself at a complete turning point because of the life that was now growing inside my womb. My upbringing, my challenges, my clinical training, my career, in essence my life experiences, had prepared me for what was to come.

There was never any question that I would put everything into being a wife and a mom. Life is about living 200 percent. I still don't cook. but I just found my honey that likes to do that. When it comes to living a life with a disability, you just acknowledge your strengths and weaknesses and create your action plan. This is a dynamic paradigm that is reassessed as needed. You must be honest with yourself for your safety and your family.

My pregnancies were absolutely wonderful. Feeling the baby move each time was a miracle. It was a moment that no one else shared except her and me. I also had the same complaints as other women and was ready for her to move out at the end.

My OB did say she could not tell me what to expect because every birth has such a range of possibilities. In my case, birth was fast and furious but natural. Gracie was born in 4 hours, and Lilly in 1 hour and 45 minutes. To this day, I cherish those experiences for their special significance. That is, I gave birth, I did it better than well, and my cerebral palsy had nothing to say about it!

The task of childcare is mastered through environmental control. In my research, I found that there are resources to help parents with adaptive equipment. We introduced an adapted crib that my husband built. It was raised to the height of my chair and the front slid open to the side so I could put the baby to bed. It had a latch on the outside so the door could not be opened by the child. For a changing table, I actually used a groomer's table as they are very sturdy and have no drawers underneath. I placed a changing pad on top and there you go; a nice convenient reason for my husband to get out of poop duty. Just as important is the removal of clutter. Children are fast and they cannot predict consequences so make sure you can move quickly without things in your way. Also anticipate that they can reach faster than you and keep those things secured.

I like to think that parenting children is helping them become who they are rather than just feeding, bathing and keeping them safe. We worked out measures of safety and consistency carefully. I changed to a power wheelchair so I could keep up with my children when they began to move and climb quickly. When it comes to parental control, my voice has always been my authority. This is a strategic decision because I want them to respect me when I speak; not because I sit in a chair, but because I am their Mama. It has been helpful in keeping them out of situations I would not be able to recover them from. For example, the children learn that I am not going to physically chase after them to enforce the rules. They also learn my tone of voice and what is a request versus what is not to be questioned. When I say "stop," "dangerous" or indicate a serious consequence, they know I mean it. We also believe in unsolicited praise and positive affirmation just because everyone should know they are valued. Finally, when it comes to discipline, we use time out or cool down time. I always take the time to discuss any incident that required discipline with my girls, talk about a better way to get what they needed, and give them an opportunity to be heard.

Motherhood has not always been easy. During Gracie's first two and a half years, she was an extreme "daddy's girl." During the day, she only depended on me for her essential needs. I would change her, feed her and drive her where she needed to go, but most of my attempts to have fun were met with cold disinterest. I was devastated. Mama didn't exist and when daddy came home, she would come alive and be a whole other child with light and life and giggles. I cried myself to sleep every night wondering how I could be such a failure at the role I had wanted since the age of twelve. I consulted her pediatrician as well as the clinical social worker to determine if I (or we) were doing something horribly wrong. No recommendations for change were made and it was never determined why her reactions were so extreme. However, when Gracie's needs became more emotional instead of romping on the floor with daddy, she began to turn to me more. I began to see what her needs were before she had the vocabulary to express them and our relationship changed. Many times, I wanted to walk away during those first two and a half years but I thought, 'I don't have the right. I asked for her to be in my life and here she is. As invisible as I felt, a child needs her Mama.' This experience, as painful as it was, taught me the most valuable lesson of parenthood. *No matter what, keep walking through the door*. Now more than three years later, Gracie does not remember rejecting me but she does say that I am her best friend. She asked me to promise that we will be this way forever.

Now that my children are a bit older, we are beginning to move into some higher reasoning. Our relationship is built on mutual respect in the way we talk to each other, the way we make agreements and carry them out and the way we get things done. I talk to them with the same respect that I would one of my parents or Rachid, for example, and as a result, they are willing to respect my authority as their parent, and we are a team.

In summary, I define childcare as doing the tasks but parenting is experiencing the moments spent with your child. It is this bridge that closes the gap of physical barriers. My creed as a mother is to involve myself in what they are doing or involve them in what I am doing. When the girls were little and there was not a playgroup in our town, I started one. When the kids learned to ride bikes, I helped them and then got a hand cycle so I could ride too. When it came to soccer, I would chase them down the field so they would run faster and then as a family we started a power soccer initiative to bring the experience of power soccer to other people in power chairs. Gracie helped Mama get her first goal and I wouldn't have wanted it any other way.

To me, being a mom and watching my children grow is an amazing gift. Lilly-bug loves me freely and completely. Gracie is genuine and enlightening. I am the lucky one to have them. It is always a series of new challenges, but you just keep walking through the door.

LESSONS TO SHARE

For Mothers with Disabilities

Acknowledge that you may not be able to do all of the physical mothering tasks but that you can still carry out the role of mothering.

Care giving includes the emotional and psychological support of your children.

Don't expect children to do the tasks involving your personal care. Do expect them to do ordinary chores. It is a desirable way to teach children how to take responsibilities.

Set up clear boundaries for the relationship of your personal care assistant—or other help you have—and your child.

For Health Care Professionals and Social Workers

Be sure that you are thinking and using "motherhood discourse" and not "disability discourse" in your relationship to a mother with a disability.

Do not assume that because the mother needs some care for her disability that she cannot be a care giver for her child.

In giving assistance to a disabled mother with her child, help her to be the mother and to carry out the tasks she is able to do.

Provide the mother with information on assistive technology (adaptive equipment) and how to use it in her circumstances.

Provide the mother with information on child welfare services if applicable.

Chapter Three

Meeting the Outside World

When do the children of a mother with a disability discover that the outside world sees her as different or odd? Phouvieng, in Part One, says her daughters hadn't noticed her disability until her youngest, at eight, saw a boy with crutches and began to ask questions. Her daughter's curiosity made Phouvieng realize it was time to talk to both girls about her disability and help them relate to other people's reactions to her.

Going to school—public or private—brings children into the mainstream of public scrutiny and challenges a disabled mother to help them place themselves in what society considers "the norm," which includes having able bodied parents. Mothers must help their children understand the power of "the norm" which falsely labels people as different and "the other" rather than accepting them as part of a desirable diversity.

Molly, in Part One, found when she wrote each parent in her son's class explaining his and her disability, that she was overwhelmed by supportive letters. Many parents shared family problems—often some kind of disability—that made them feel outside the norm. She realized there were few "normal" families.

But children might not understand these realities when they are confronted, as Phouvieng's children were, with classmates who teased them about their mother being "a midget." They need guidance and, as Sara Ruddick (1995), the scholar of "maternal thinking" argues, a mother's role is not only to protect and preserve but also to teach values.

Sometimes, specific lessons are emphasized by mothers, particularly in minority groups. Cheryl Najarian (2006) in her book *Between Worlds*, about deaf mothers, explains that the mothers are often placed "between two worlds" where they want to teach their children how to live in the deaf community of ASL, but also the hearing society. As she writes, "[The deaf

mothers] had to teach their children the art of going back and forth between
these two worlds and to be proud of deaf culture as part of their family and
balance that within the context of a larger hearing community" (p.19).

Patricia Hill Collins (1991) in *Black Feminist Thought*, writes of the
mother daughter relationship. Growing from the need to resist oppression,
black mothers teach their daughters "the tools for survival" and "integrated
self-reliance with motherhood." Collins writes that although mothers wish to
provide a better chance for advancement for their daughters, they must also
provide protection and lessons for physical survival (pp.120-130).

Speaking to an adult audience of both able-bodied and disabled people,
Rosemarie Garland Thomson (2009) in *Staring: How We Look* particularly
challenges people with disabilities to teach the rest of the world to reevaluate
"the norm" and learn how to see "the other." Garland Thomson takes on the
complex process of how we look at one another, including the encounter of
staring. She explains that the staring relationship can be "an intense visual
exchange that makes meaning" and that can broaden "the collective expectations of who can and should be seen in the public sphere" (p. 9). Those of us
with disabilities, she argues, have an obligation to make the relationship
positive, even transformative.

After an analysis of the aspects of the relationship between the starer and
the staree, Thomson examines some of the successful strategies that starees,
particularly disabled people, have developed to teach others how to look at
them so they can better understand human differences. She uses the example
of Harriet McBryde Johnson, disability rights lawyer and storyteller.
McBryde, best known for her debate with Peter Singer over the question of
euthanasia and the right of parents to euthanize disabled children, appeared
on the cover of the New York Times magazine (February 16, 2003) in her
wheelchair. The cover photo and another photograph of her with her article
shows the severe effects of the neuromuscular disease McBryde had since
birth. If this were a personal encounter, the able bodied person would probably be staring. Thomson points out how McBride in her article confronts her
readers with her own description of her disabled body:

> The sight of me is routinely discombobulating. At this stage of my life, I am
> Karen Carpenter thin, flesh mostly vanished, a jumble of bones in a floppy bag
> of skin (New York Times Magazine, p.52).

She goes on, however, to claim her body:

> At fifteen, I threw away the back brace and let my spine reshape itself into a
> deep twisty S-curve. Now my right side is two deep canyons. To keep myself
> upright, I lean forward, rest my rib cage on my lap, plant my elbows beside my
> knees.

Finally McBryde expresses "comfort" with her body (and by extension, her life): "Since my backbone found its own natural shape, I've been entirely comfortable in my skin."

Thomson describes McBryde's strategy of teaching her audience how to look at her distinctiveness as turning something "harrowing" to most people into something ordinary. In other words, Thomson writes, "She gets [her readers] accustomed to looking at her by making herself more familiar than strange, by bringing her life story closer to their own (p. 191). The encounter, Thomson concludes, can be transformative. Thomson also points out that this story is just part of McBryde's strategy in media and public appearances to coach the public how to look at her and learn how to encounter "different" people.

All the disabled women interviewed in this project were committed to helping their children understand and navigate the outside world. Recognizing that their children might face at best curiosity and at worst, discrimination because of having a disabled mother or parent, they tried to be proactive in connecting with their children's classes and school and social activities. Julie wrote an illustrated book for her son's class about their "family" with the mother in a wheelchair. Kate talked about her disability to her daughter's classes. Tammy and others participated in their children's activities and school events.

Many of the women also confronted the public world and stood up against discrimination. Lily, whose story follows, is a model of activism and advocacy for her daughter. She defies prejudice and questions society's imposition of a "norm" that excludes others, including people with disabilities. She is determined to teach the able bodied world to accept people with disabilities as equals.

1. ENCOUNTERING THE WORLD: A ROLE MODEL

Lily: We all have something to teach other people

Lily, born in 1969 in Fresno, California. suffered a spinal cord injury from an accident at twenty-two when her truck hit black ice and went out of control on a hill. She was five months pregnant and her husband was overseas in the Gulf war.

In the hospital and the rehabilitation center, Lily found that the doctors considered her a full quadriplegic and they did not expect her to walk again. Another spinal cord injury patient told her she would always be in a wheelchair. All of the doctors said, "Well, you're going to put your child up for adoption, aren't you?" Lily felt that society in general agreed that she would not be able to raise a child.

She herself wondered, "How am I going to do this? How am I going to have this child and take care of her? "She describes her condition. "My hands were not working. They were curled up. I could not lift anything. I could not even scratch my nose." But she was determined to keep her child and walk again. She told the doctors, "I will be back. I will be back walking. It may not be on my own, but with a walker, and I will bring her [my daughter]." She continues, "And that was one thing I did. I did go back, and I did show them all. And a lot of them admitted, 'You said you were going to do it. We didn't believe you, and well, you did it. You proved us wrong.'"

Lily uses a walker outside, drives a car and has a wheelchair for use at home. She feels that after she gave birth much of the pressure on her spinal cord was relieved and may have contributed to some of her recovery. But she also says, "It's just a miracle! That's the only way I can put it."

Lily combines a spirit of determination and faith. She has become an inspiration for her family and many others, particularly mothers who are disabled. Her husband, who has always been supportive, says she is "stubborn and strong-headed and that's a good thing. Because it's gotten her where she is." Lily says he would come home on leave whenever he could—sometimes only a few days—but he read all the information on her disability and never pitied her. He said to others, "She's still the same person I fell in love with in high school. She just gets around differently. I'm amazed at what she can do. She's very independent."

Lily's independence has taken her, as her husband noted, to stubbornness at times. When she started to drive again, she insisted that she drive an ordinary car—not one specially modified for her disability—as the Department of Motor Vehicles required. It took her four years to convince them to give her a license. She would pass the tests but they wouldn't give her the license unless she modified her car. Finally, they compromised and issued a license on the condition that she return every year for a driving test.

Lily was lucky that her parents were totally supportive of her keeping and raising her child. She says their attitude was "You can do it. Whatever you set your mind to, you can do it, and if you can't we'll help you if we can." Her father made their home accessible so she could stay there when she came from the hospital with her infant daughter. Her mother was ready to help but she also encouraged Lily to learn to manage on her own and improvise. Lily says her attitude was "She's your daughter; she's my granddaughter. And that's it."

Like the other mothers in this book, Lily did learn how to manage on her own. Her mother was there when needed—to take her to the doctor, for instance, but she let Lily be the mother. Lily remembers when she returned from the hospital with her daughter:

She was so small she couldn't fit in the crib. So, she was put in a little shoebox. She was so tiny. She didn't even weigh five pounds. I figured out everything— how to dress her, bathe her. I did it from a wheelchair. I learned how to take the side of the crib down when she finally did get in a crib. I would lean over with my chin and kind of knock her over on her side, so I could fasten her clothing, but I was very careful.

Lily: Is she a normal child?

Lily is angry when she remembers that some people felt she could not raise her child adequately and would even ask about Miriam, "Is she a normal child?" as if Lily's disability was catching. And they didn't expect her to be able to be active for her daughter in school. Lily is defiant:

She [Miriam] did not lack anything. Did she miss out on anything? No, she did not miss out on anything. Just because I'm disabled I didn't tell her you can't do that because mommy's disabled. I volunteered as homeroom mom, PTA, everything through kindergarten on up. I've been active from day one. And I still am active because that's part of being a parent.

The teachers, she said, were amazed at her commitment and activities. They said a lot of parents who don't have disabilities didn't make the effort.

Lily: Describe normal to me

Lily taught the school children about disabilities. Often it was their parents who were judgmental and ill informed. She even heard a parent tell her curious child not to talk to "that lady" or ask questions. "She's not normal," she said. Lily gave her a piece of her mind:

I said, excuse me, why are you telling her that? How do you think children learn? They ask questions. And who are you to say what is normal in society? Describe normal to me. And she couldn't. I said, I'm normal, just as you. It's just that I use a chair or a walker for my legs.

In this encounter with the curious child and rebuking mother, Lily is practicing what Rosemarie Garland-Thomson in her book *Staring* would call "visual activism. " She is using her disability, which makes her different from the "normal" person, to teach the mother and child how to look at and understand her difference and by implication all differences in others. First of all, she sees the child's curiosity and staring as good and natural for a child who seeks to know the world. Then she rejects the word "normal" which the mother used about Lily and challenges her to define the word, which, she cannot do. Having disrupted the mother's notion of "normal," she redefines it as covering a broader concept, one that includes someone who uses a wheel-chair or a walker and then all of those who have a disability.

This "teaching" of the able bodied world (and by example her daughter) is consistent throughout Lily's narrative. She rejects expectations of doctors and even a fellow patient that she will never walk after her accident and she refuses to accept the standard requirements of the Registry of Motor Vehicles that she cannot drive an unadapted car.

I asked Lily if she had any impact on the parents at the school and she said she did. They'd eventually come up and ask her about her accident and offer to help her in any way. And she'd explain that she was managing fine but that they needed to learn about disability and how it affects everybody and to learn how to treat a disabled person like every human being. And just as Molly in Part One had discovered that parents confided in her about their own family disabilities, Lily found parents would confide in her about a loved one who had some kind of illness or accident or disability. One mother was grateful when Lily made a special effort to speak to her child, who had a disability.

> *Later she saw me in a store, and came up and said 'Thank you so much." And I said, Why? And she replied 'For actually talking to my child and not running away'. Why wouldn't I? I said. Your daughter is a beautiful daughter. And the mother said, 'You just made my day.'*

Because her husband was often away in the service, Lily says, "I was a single parent. I would be me on my own with her. But we knew I could deal with that job." She often had to make parenting decisions by herself, such as how to discipline her daughter.

When someone asked her how she could discipline Miriam from a wheel-chair, she explained that when Miriam was young she would get spankings. "She knew what she did wrong. She'd come back and say, 'I'm really sorry. I'm not going to do that again.' And I'd talk about it. But that kind of gets old." Lily says she had to find new ways to keep her daughter in line as she grew up. She explains her approach.

> *Well, let's see. Now she's a teenager. What do teenage girls love doing? They love being on the phone; they love being on the computer; they love all of their little knick-knacks. That's how I discipline her. I take things that she really loves away from her for a while. And she's grounded to this house. Then when she can appreciate it, she gets her little luxuries back.*

One question Lily asks herself is whether she gave her daughter too much responsibility as a child. The question bothers her at times as she looks back at her daughter's years growing up.

Miriam grew up a whole lot faster than a child her age should have. She felt she had to help mommy a lot. I'm not going to say I did not ask her to help me a lot when it was just she and I. She matured a lot faster and she took on a little bit more responsibility than I really wanted her to take on, which is my fault.

Lily reflects that being a mother with a disability is very hard: "I tell my daughter 'Being a parent is the hardest job.' There is no such thing as a perfect parent. And there are a lot of books out there about parenting. But there are no books on parenting and disability. I'd like to hear about how others handle some of these questions."

I asked Lily if her daughter discussed her disability with her and whether Miriam's friends asked her about it. Lily says Miriam is very comfortable about talking to her about her disability and Miriam's friends are comfortable, too.

There's no problem about her [Miriam] talking about it at all. I'm just a mommy. She knows I have a disability but that doesn't bother her. All the kids that she has grown up with are aware of my disability. When she meets someone new and they want to know what happened to me, Miriam explains, 'My mommy is disabled. She has a spinal cord injury.' And then she explains more. And they'll usually say, 'Wow! she's got a cool looking wheelchair. Can I take a little ride in it?'

Lily has become an advocate for the disabled. She was asked to speak at the rehabilitation center for teenage girls with spinal cord injuries and to give them a pep talk on recovery. Lily explains what she told them:

I said, I know what they told you. You're never going to walk again. I said, well, you know what? That can be proven wrong. I said, if you can wiggle a thumb or an index finger or any of your little toes, you're on your way. I said, if you really want it, you can work at it. You have to work at it.

Not surprisingly, the girls wanted to know if they could have children and have a sex life. Again Lily gave them frank and hopeful answers:

I said, there is nothing wrong with your reproductive organs. You're going to have your menstrual cycle. You can have a sex life. And you know what, it doesn't have to be with someone who is in a chair either. It can be an able bodied gentleman. But it's going to take a very special person, who's going to love you and understand what you've been through and go through a process with you. But you can have a life. You can have a family.

Lily's advocacy and support has reached out to many. She insists, "We have rights, just like everybody else. We have the right to be heard." She also says, "People with disabilities have come a long way/"

She communicates with other women with spinal cord injuries on the internet as well as those whom she's met locally. And she's always eager to make new acquaintances with people with other disabilities and to keep up with old friends.

Lily acknowledges,

> *I love talking and meeting people. I'm always amazed at other people's situations and how they overcome barriers. I'm just curious. My husband—he laughs at me. He says, 'You're a busybody.' I'm not a busybody! I just love meeting different people. I just really do. Other people are interesting!*

But she also insists that people with disabilities have to speak out and be heard. They have to reach out to others: "We [the disabled] have so much to give to other people. That's if they are willing to sit and listen. And to learn and not just judge the outside appearances of people."

Lily is a role model for her daughter as well as for others.

2. NEGOTIATING FOR TWO: WHEN YOUR CHILD ALSO HAS A DISABILITY

Six of the mothers interviewed have a child with a disability: three inherited their mother's genetic condition: Molly's son inherited Hereditary Spastic Paraplegia, Laura's daughter inherited her mother's type of dwarfism. In addition, Ellen's first son is partially blind from premature birth, Beatrice's daughter has Down Syndrome and Phouvieng's youngest daughter has type one diabetes.

Ellen's and Beatrice's stories are about mothers with disabilities who negotiate for their disabled children.

Ellen: I really believe [my son's premature birth] could have been prevented had my doctors kept a closer eye on my pregnancy and I had more educated practitioners

Ellen, born in 1979, has a spinal cord injury from a car accident when she was twenty-three and driving under the influence of alcohol. She uses a wheelchair but has mobility in her arms and the upper part of her body. She met her husband in a 12 Step Recovery Program in Little Rock, Arkansas, joined the Twelve Step Program and has been sober since 2002. They have two sons. One of them is blind in the left eye.

I interviewed Ellen twice, once when her sons were two and five months old and again when they were five and almost three. Initially, she spoke about her adjustment to her disability and her experiences with giving birth and becoming a mother. Later, she described her progress and her success as a working mom and what it means to her to have a child with a disability. She also spoke of the goals and hopes she and her husband have for their sons as they grow up.

"One of the first things I asked after I was injured, Ellen says, is 'Will I be able to have children'? My doctor said yes, and I was encouraged. I planned to wait a while and finish school and do other stuff. But nobody told me I shouldn't have children."

Ellen hadn't quite expected to have her first child so soon after she married, two years after the accident. She was almost immediately pregnant, not being able to use birth control because of the danger of blood clots. Her family was at first concerned and scared for her but "after they got over the initial shock they were happy."

Ellen thinks that her first son's disability—Retinopathy of Prematurity— was probably the result of her doctor's lack of knowledge about how her disability would affect her pregnancy and delivery, particularly related to her being paralyzed from the waist down. She remembers her delivery:

> There were issues in the first pregnancy that weren't addressed. They didn't check my cervix frequently. I went into labor fifteen weeks early. I thought I was having Braxton Hicks (false) contractions, but I was actually having real contractions. They lost the heart beats [there were twins] on the monitor. And it was just terrible. Finally one doctor thought to check my cervix. And our son was already out. That's when they rushed and everybody flooded the room. It was just shear panic.

Her son was born fifteen weeks early at one pound eleven ounces. As a result, he has ROP (Retinopathy Prematurity) and is blind in the left eye and has low vision and poor visual acuity in the other eye.

During that delivery, Ellen lost their little twin girl, delivered by c-section. She describes the painful memory when she and her husband went over to see her daughter, who had been taken to another hospital. Ellen said it was very hard. She says, "I guess the reason that I've dealt with it is because of the way she looked when we saw her. She looked like she was in pain and she was suffering. I'm glad she didn't have to go through more of that."

Ellen's second pregnancy was less than two years after her first son's birth. This time she sought out a high risk obstetrician and things went well. She says, "This doctor had worked with paralyzed women before. So we put our heads together and were able to keep the pregnancy going for thirty-seven weeks." Her second child, a healthy baby boy, was delivered by c-section because she wanted to have her tubes tied. Ellen says that some day they would like to adopt a little girl.

Erik, her first son, has had a lot of "medical stuff," Ellen says. He's had a virectomy, PDA ligation and bilateral hernia repair. Karl, the younger one, at six months, was the same size that Erik was at fifteen months. Both children were in day care from the time they were babies. Karl was in one section, "the Hummingbird," and Erik in another. Erik received special therapies: occupational, physical, developmental and speech therapy.

Ellen: He's [Erik] progressed so much. He's very smart

In our first interview, Ellen spoke of how pleased she and her husband were that Erik, who was then three, had made such progress. "He has progressed so much. He's very smart. He surprised us every day, because he's just now started to talk and his level of understanding is almost at his chronological age."

Ellen, like all the other mothers, has found ways to adapt and improvise in caring for her children. But her sons have also adapted to her. One of her most thrilling moments was when Erik started walking. "He started crawling up on my lap. The wheelchair was an issue for him. And so it's been really neat to see how compassionate he is and how indifferent he is toward my disability."

Ellen appreciates the fact that her husband helps her a lot but he also pushes her to do what she can. "He doesn't enable me in any way and it kind of keeps me strong and independent and feeling more—I hate to use the word normal—but that's really what it is!" When the children were little, her husband gave Erik his bath and fed him breakfast and took the children to day care every day. Ellen primarily took care of the baby. Now, she says, they continue to work well together. "It's a partnership."

Ellen was able to start college courses again soon after Karl was born and she became active—giving talks—in both AA and in the Spinal Cord Injury Association. She also reaches out to other women with disabilities and belongs to several disability groups on MySpace where she has a blog. She has found that she can be helpful to other women with disabilities.

> I've found that not only just women in wheelchairs but that disabled women in general are able to discuss things that other people just don't understand. I've had a lot of girls contact me through MySpace and ask me about sex and what you can and can't do and about family life and my relationship with my husband. And they also ask about parenting, too.

Like so many of the mothers in this group, Ellen puts a lot of energy into proving to the world that not only can she take care of her children but that, because she is disabled, she has much to teach them. She feels that she is able to fulfill her role as a mother completely and she speaks passionately about it:

> There is nothing lacking in my role, and I don't think that some people understand that. There's a lot that I bring to the table in my relationship with my

husband and my relationship with my children that I don't think that a lot of other parents can teach their children. My children will be able to understand that no matter what your disability, you're still a whole person. And, you know, other parents, I don't think, really face the situations we do. I'm able to go over bumps smoothly and other parents might balk at some of the stuff.

At the end of the first interview, Ellen said that her quality of life, since her accident, has actually gotten much better. She is no longer an alcoholic and sick all the time and she has a good marriage and two wonderful sons. Furthermore, she has a heightened sense of compassion toward other people since she has been disabled, particularly those who suffer misfortune in some way.

In our second interview, almost three years after the first one, Ellen has seen a number of changes in her life. She has become a successful working mother and her sons are in school. Erik is in a special school, "The Arkansas School for the Blind," named before the public was sensitive to a relationship to people with disabilities that did not lump them together in institutionalized groups. Karl, the younger son, is in pre-school, situated very close to Ellen's office in Little Rock

"I love the job that I do." says Ellen. She works in an office that manages justice assistance grants and other federal grants and has been involved in applying for and managing recent federal stimulus money.

Ellen feels she has been very lucky in finding a job. After she completed a B.A. in liberal arts, which emphasized Communication and writing courses, and after volunteering to write grants with the Spinal Cord Association's grant program, she heard of the job working on stimulus money through a good friend of her mother's, a state senator. He passed on her resume and she was given an interview. Ellen acknowledges her good fortune: "He actually helped me get the interview. And, luckily, I didn't have to go through that process of not knowing anybody and having to go to the interview and let them know I'm disabled."

Ellen is also quick to say that she got *herself* the job from the interview and then after proving herself at work, got a permanent job that opened up.

Her husband is now the student so they are quite dependent on Ellen's income, but they are managing and it is clear that she feels confident in herself and has been able to advance in her job. She acknowledges that it is one of the best times of her life. She and her husband have overcome many obstacles and they have a good relationship. "We spend a lot more time together than most of my friends who are married. Partly because he helps me, but we work well together."

I asked her if her sons notice her disability. The two boys, not surprisingly, interact differently with her about her disability and her being in a wheelchair. Erik, her five year old, is particularly sensitive to her impairments because he is aware of his own. She says, "Erik, my five year old, knows that I had a car accident, that I have a spinal cord injury, and that the message doesn't get up to my brain and that's why I can't walk."

He also knows quite a bit about his own disability and he is curious about it. Ellen explains: "Last year he asked us to take him up to the hospital where he was for three and a half months, and he wanted to know what kind of bed he was in."

Karl, the three year old, Ellen says, has been asking her about her disability and sometimes refers to "when you walk again." She has to explain that she doesn't know if that's ever going to happen. And says, "This is just who I am." And she adds, "For the most part, he's perfectly fine with it.

The two boys' schools represent quite an educational contrast —an institution that is run entirely for children who are disabled and a preschool that does not have any disabled children and, as Ellen noted, has primarily Caucasian children, mostly from the suburbs.

At Erik's school the children are diverse and disabled in some way. Several children have multiple disabilities and several use walkers or are in wheelchairs. "All the children," Ellen says, "are very aware of the assistive technology that is used." Ellen is happy about the school, at least at this point in her son's life. He has small classes, they go on weekly field trips and his teacher is very available and is regularly in touch by email, addressing any questions or concerns Ellen might have.

> *I think it's the right place for [Erik] to be. I was a little concerned, and I think my family was even more concerned, about him being too segregated from normal kids. But I think because he had some severe developmental delays for a long time, he should stay there now, probably until third grade.*

Karl goes to a Pentecostal preschool—although Ellen and her husband are not Pentecostal. They like the teachers and the curriculum. The children are naturally curious about her wheelchair and want to climb around it and under it, which, as Ellen says, is very normal. She finds that she does not interact much with the other parents, whom she feels don't know quite how to approach her. "I think they really don't know how to interact until I start talking to them and then they're okay with it."

When Erik is seven or eight and Karl is about five, Ellen plans to get her boys involved with organizations, such as Easter Seals, that work with the disability community so they can learn about different kinds of disabilities. She says "I really have in my heart [the desire] to get involved in volunteering to do community work with [my sons]. That's a big goal of mine."

She continues, "I think without even teaching them, I'm showing them that I can do almost everything that moms can do and that no matter what the adverse situation that they face, they'll be able to get through it."

Her relationship with her husband shows them "that people need each other and can work well together, regardless of whether they have a disability or not."

Lily and Ellen both want to show the world and their children that they function fully as mothers and that people with disabilities should be treated as equals to everyone. They have different circumstances and in some cases, different approaches. One of their differences is apparent in the way they use the word "normal" in telling their stories. Lily lectured her fellow parent on the misuse of the word. Ellen is apologetic when she uses the word in explaining that her husband enables her to be independent and makes her feel—I hate to use the word, but that's what it is—more "normal." Later she refers to "normal" children as opposed to disabled children in school. Ellen's ambivalence in the use of the word could be the result of her having experienced a recovery from alcoholism and its demand of constant vigilance in keeping on track; she is more aware of a normative standard she must keep for wellness. At the same time, she is sensitive to the judgment of the public with their stares at her difference as a paraplegic and to her son's future challenges with his disability. Ellen keeps a fine balance and has embraced a goal for all of her family to reach out to others in need without judging them.

Beatrice: The school system pretty much ignored me. I didn't even get to a classroom

Beatrice, born in the Azores in 1956, is legally blind. She has sought access to quality education, at first for herself and now for her daughter, who has Down Syndrome. Being very confident in her capabilities as a person and mother, she tries to reassure the world of her capabilities. Her daughter is ten and she has a son, who is seven.

Beatrice's disability was the result of a case of measles after she was hospitalized at seven with pneumonia. She was given a blood transfusion and had a bad reaction called Stevens-Johnson Syndrome. Her blindness was the result of this reaction. Recently, she has had eye surgery that has improved her vision somewhat.

Her parents, in contrast to cultural practices in the Azores, did not treat her like a disabled child. They had expectations for her which, she says, shaped her approach to her own expectations for herself. However, although she was sent to school, "they didn't know how to teach me. They didn't have a way to teach a child who was visually impaired." When she came to this country in 1972, she expected the schools would be different and could accommodate her, but she was disappointed. "The school system pretty much ignored me. I didn't even get to a classroom."

Beatrice ended up staying home and doing the housework and the baby-sitting for the family. Her break came when she was sent by the school system to the Perkins School for the Blind for vocational training and an English teacher there saw her potential and began to teach her English and other subjects. With the help of other teachers, Beatrice got her GED (General Education Diploma), went to Framingham State College for a B.A, and eventually got a master's degree in Social Work from Boston College.

Beatrice married and when her daughter was born, she experienced a skeptical attitude about her ability to care for a child. She was shocked because she had not only grown up taking care of children for her family, but she was also a social worker who had advised families with disabled members. The social worker at the hospital expressed concern and asked what supports she would have at home to help her. Beatrice says she felt awful and cried when she told her husband. She says, "I knew I didn't have any limitations physically preventing me from caring for my daughter. That's the only time I really felt they were doubting my capability of taking care of my child,"

Now Beatrice reflects, "Some social workers are really not that great! They lack sensitivity. Like any profession, there are good ones and not so good ones. And I experienced that." Before her son was born, she had changed doctors and hospitals and things were much better. Her husband stayed home a week to help her and after that she was on her own with the baby. Her daughter went to preschool a few hours every day. Beatrice says she "felt very comfortable around the house."

In the outside world, Beatrice sensed that some people were uncomfortable seeing her with her children when she used a white cane. Ellen and Lily had similar experiences from their wheelchairs. Beatrice specifically mentioned the parents of her children's friends who initially wanted to stay when they brought their children to play, but later became comfortable in leaving their children.

Beatrice's attitude toward these reactions is very laid back:

> I don't let it bother me too much. I show them that I'm quite capable as a visually impaired person. That's always been my strategy pretty much with society as a whole. I just do my thing and don't get too concerned. I tell my kids' friends, 'You're welcome to come. You're welcome to leave.'' Some parents will drop their kids. You can tell they're comfortable. Other parents will stick around. Which is fine with me. It's sort of their personal discomfort with a disability. Once they get a little more comfortable, they'll leave their kids.

Sometimes her children's friends asked, "What's wrong with your mommy's eyes?" Her son, particularly, didn't know what to say so Beatrice explained why her eyes "don't work very well." Beatrice says, "It's usually with young kids. It's just curiosity."

Her daughter, Beatrice says, is very empathetic to her mother's disability. She is intuitive and loves to feel she is helping. "If I asked her where something was, she would take my hand. Without anyone telling her what to do, she would just take my hand and say 'Hey, Mom, it's right here.' Or she would put my hand on the outfit I was looking for and take me to it, saying, 'It's right here Mommy.'"

Beatrice remembers that when her children were younger, they did take advantage of her sometimes. Particularly her daughter, who figured she could hide out "in plain sight."

Beatrice would tell them, "I can gauge where you guys are. I can see you guys even if I can't see you guys." Her son once said, "Mommy, you're not a superhero. You're just a mommy." But she responded, "Yeah, but I'm a mommy with super powers!"

Beatrice is very involved in her children's school. She and her husband go to many meetings. She's gone on field trips, too. However, she doesn't think the school system does as much as it could for children with special needs. She says, "I don't think in general schools have a lot of expectations for kids with special needs."

She feels that her daughter, who is mainstreamed in a third grade, has a lot of untapped potential:

> *I don't think the school is tapping into her potential. I don't think they push her as much as they should. You know, challenging her. They modify her work. Give her very simple stuff to do. I see the stuff that she does at home. And I've talked to them. I've said, you know she is a good learner in a lot of ways. I keep talking to the school about it.*

Beatrice also has some disagreements about whether or not it is wise to hold back her daughter a year if she is not meeting standards. She repeated kindergarten and Beatrice feels it would be better to hold her back again if she is not ready to go to the next level. The school disagrees, arguing that it would be bad for her daughter's self esteem. But Beatrice feels that her daughter is socially quite mature and confident—"she's good with kids and adults" and would not be upset by repeating a grade. On the other hand, Beatrice says, she is not mature academically. "In a lot of ways she is not what a ten year old is."

Beatrice is sure that her daughter can get through high school—and she thinks the school has that goal, too—but she would like to see her have some post high school education. "She's very determined. Something she wants to do, she's going to do it. She finds a way to do it." But Beatrice doesn't think the school has that kind of hope for her daughter.

A group of parents with special needs children from other schools have met from time to time to talk about similar issues. Beatrice has found it helpful. "You feel you are not alone," she says. However, they have found that the school system gets very defensive if they make suggestions. "Sometimes, it makes things worse so you have to be very careful. We feel that we better not rock the boat too much. It's very political."

As a social worker, Beatrice has had a wide range of experience with different kinds of people, who don't always fit into the "normal" pattern. She has worked with adults who were blind and mentally challenged and she feels she learned a lot from that experience. She has also worked with Portuguese speaking adults and has tried to help them bridge cultural gaps, often between generations in their own families:

> *Families come here with children or have children here and the children learn the culture very quickly. They go to school and learn the language and the culture. And sometimes the kids use that to their advantage against the parents.*

As an example, Beatrice cited the cultural differences about disciplining children. The immigrant parents, learning from their own parents, are likely to discipline their child with spanking and the child might say "No, that is not the way they do it in America" and even report it to a teacher:

> *The child tells the teacher 'My parent hit me.' And then the Social Services are involved, and the parents are in shock. If you're from a different culture that is a little more rigid and less open about things, an agency that protects the rights of children is not something you grew up with and you wonder, 'Who are these people?'*

Beatrice feels discipline "is such a fine line." She uses the "time out" way but she understands that some parents don't think it works. But consistency, she says, is the most important thing, and setting limits. "Kids act out and that's why they need those limits. Limits are so important. Sometimes, it is the easy way out to give in and do whatever they want, but in the long run, it is not the thing to do. Children need to learn their limits in life."

"Parenting is one of the hardest jobs I've ever done, " Beatrice says. But she would advise women with disabilities to have children if they think they can do it. She says, "I don't think they should be told that they can't be mothers just because they are in a wheelchair or because they are blind." Beyond the physical tasks of mothering, Beatrice says, "Being a mother is to be there for them. To be there when they fall. Give them a hug, Talk to them and explain things to them and read to them. Anybody in a wheelchair can do the same thing I can do."

Beatrice also believes that much more could be done to help parents with disabilities. In her case, she would like more resources to help blind parents.

For instance, she needs to help her daughter with her homework and cannot find any resources to help her.

> *There is nothing out there to help me. Give me guidance, you know. I looked, but there is nothing available. And I said, dear God, there are blind parents out there who have kids in school, so how come there is nothing? There used to be a parenting magazine from the Mass Association for the Blind, but apparently they've stopped.*

More resources. Better awareness of the needs of disabled mothers and parents in helping their children. Many of the women interviewed echoed these challenges.

3. GROWING UP IN A SPECIAL COMMUNITY

Patti, who is partially sighted, lived with her husband, also visually impaired, and their two children at the Perkins School for the Blind for ten years. Their two able bodied children grew up in the community where a disability was "the norm" and although they went eventually to private schools outside the community, they are comfortable with a world that is both able bodied and disabled.

Patti, born in 1941, is legally blind from a brain tumor on her optic nerve. She lost her sight in the left eye and also her sense of taste and smell. Surgery was not completely successful in removing the tumor and, she says, she sees less well now than when her children were born.

Patti's family never thought of her as visually impaired and encouraged her to continue her education. She went to Boston University as an undergraduate and received a master's degree in special education. She taught kindergarten in the public school system before becoming a teacher at Perkins. More recently, she volunteers at Perkins and participates in an international a capella chorus and square dancing.

Patti met her husband, Mike, at Perkins when they were both teachers there and they were married at the Perkins chapel. They have been a team in many years of living and working at Perkins. Mike says of Patti, "She's all about family. She's my hero."

At first Patti's parents were upset when she wished to marry someone who was blind and a Catholic! But they were won over, says Patti, by "my outgoing, sociable Italian husband!"

In contrast to Patti's background growing up, Mike, as a child, experienced discrimination in elementary school from the nuns who thought he was mentally challenged until they diagnosed his visual impairment in fourth grade. His poor reading skills kept him from college until a doctor introduced him to a Keeler Magnifier, which enabled him to read and then to catch up on his education. He graduated from Boston University with a B.S. in Physical Education and later a Master's degree. He became head of Physical Education and the Athletic Program at Perkins and is now Coordinator of Volunteer Services and has been honored widely for his outstanding work in volunteerism.

When Patti and her husband were first married they enjoyed a warm sense of community at Perkins where they lived in a campus apartment for seven years and then in Perkins housing for three years until they bought their own house nearby. The Perkins School, started in 1829, has a rich history as the first school for the blind in the United States and as a pioneer in innovative instructional techniques. Its famous students, Laura Bridgman, the first known deafblind person to be educated, and the more famous Helen Keller helped to break down barriers about what people who are blind or deafblind can accomplish.

Her husband, Patti says, loves cooking and company and gathering friends at home so their children were surrounded with friends who took their parents' blindness for granted. In fact, says Patti, she did not experience a negative attitude from the world toward her as a mother who is blind—she uses a cane for identification. Rather, she found that most people's reaction was very positive when she was with her children and they would often comment, "Aren't you great to manage!"

The main strategy that Patti used in managing her household, she says, was to be very organized. Every thing had its place and stayed there. Otherwise, mistakes could be made, she says, such as when she almost cooked with Clorox instead of oil or when she used Four Seasons tea instead of spices! Her microwave is equipped with Braille, which Patti learned, and her gas stove top clicks for off and on.

Comparing Patti's experience with Beatrice's, it seems that the inclusiveness of the Perkins community and perhaps its extended social network, provided Patti and her family with an enlightened and protective embrace. However, Patti is aware that there are many problems for disabled mothers. She mentioned that she was part of a group of visually impaired mothers, who met as a support group at Perkins. It was started by a social worker after one of her clients had a disturbing experience. A neighbor saw the mother getting help from her younger child in lifting the baby and called Social Services to report her as endangering her child.

Nor does Patti claim that she had no issues managing her children, particularly when they were small. Her daughter, she says, was quite "rambunctious—a hellion" as a small child. Patti remembers that her daughter did occasionally take advantage of her. For instance, knowing her mother could not see her, once her daughter climbed up on the counter and got the sugar scoop, taking it into the dining room and leaving a trail of sugar behind her. Patti found that sending her to pre-school helped. Her daughter was also the more rebellious teenager, Patti says, and she went through a time when she resented the limitations she felt because her parents couldn't drive and take her places. Now, however, her daughter, obviously influenced by the Perkins community experience, is an interpreter for the deaf in Portland, Maine. She has two little girls of her own, for whom Patti loves to babysit. Her son, influenced by Mike's passion for sports, is a hockey coach at a college.

Patti's children were able to go to private school and college on scholarships so they were often outside the Perkins community. However, both children were significantly affected and shaped by growing up as part of that community. They are both comfortable in the able-bodied world as well as the disabled world. Patti has also been very active outside of the Perkins community, giving talks to various organizations about the work at Perkins and about the visually impaired community. She also attends plays and movies with audio description for the visually impaired.

In her pioneering collection of writings about parenting by mothers with disabilities, Michele Wates (1999) confronts this question of normality. Faced with her own challenges from multiple sclerosis after she had her second child, she confesses that she gets the sense that disabled mothers are assumed to be "problem mothers." She counters with the assertion that her feeling is, on the contrary, that "there are certain distinctive strengths in the parenting styles of disabled people" and after meeting with many disabled mothers she poses the question:

> *Are our families characterized by their normality or by their exceptionality? Are we concerned with merging into the mainstream or are we signaling a way forward; creating styles of parenting that are less isolated, more comfortable with difference and that richly foster the skills of interdependence?* (pp. 95-96).

LESSONS TO SHARE

For Mothers with Disabilities

Become engaged in your children's school activities. Participate in classes, events, forums. PTA, other parent groups.

Discuss with your children the reaction of other children to you as a disabled mother. Explain how society often imposes an arbitrary "norm" which excludes people with disabilities.

Discuss your disability with your children, sharing medical information if it seems appropriate to their age or interest.

Be a role model: show the power of overcoming obstacles; be an advocate for the acceptance of differences.

For Health Care Professionals and Social Workers

Recognize a disabled mother's special gifts: ingenuity, adaptability, creativity, determination.

Recognize the actual advantages of being a child of a mother with a disability: a child learns to be more responsible for themselves; a child becomes more sensitive to other "stigmatized" individuals; a child is more tolerant of diversity.

Acknowledge that the general public and even neighbors may be ignorant or fearful of a disabled mother's capabilities in caring for her children. Help the disabled mother to negotiate these relationships and encounters.

Chapter Four

Family Relationships and Community

We need to reconceptualize care [given to children] to include aspects of mutuality and reciprocity (Mullin 2005)

1. HOW MUCH HELP SHOULD CHILDREN GIVE THEIR DISABLED PARENTS?

Communications across the media—whether print articles or internet blogs or TV sitcoms or dramas—often reflect the question that many parents ask themselves: how much should I expect my children to contribute to the running of the family household? Answers vary greatly. Some parents provide extensive job schedules, others pay their children to perform tasks and some ask their children to contribute very little or nothing to household routines. Disabled parents ask the same questions and often have the same answers.

A recent study of parents with disabilities—sixty-two per cent of them mothers—and their teens found "that teenage children do the same number of chores, have the same number of friends and keep the same bedtime schedule as teens whose parents don't have disabilities." In short, the study concluded that "parents with disabilities raising teens are more like than unlike parents without disabilities" (Barbara and Jim Twardowsk 2005).

Most of the mothers interviewed here expect their children to do some tasks at home, such as keeping their rooms in order. For instance, Phouvieng, whose story was in Part One, believed her two daughters should be assigned regular household chores and she made a schedule for them to keep. However, most of these mothers agree that they do not ask their children to help them with personal needs.

Sometimes children do take on a considerable amount of responsibility in helping a disabled parent. Between 1992 and 1998 in Great Britain the phenomena of children "parenting the parent" became identified as a social problem by social scientists and healthcare professionals. The debate was shaped by negative assumptions about the parenting capacities of people with disabilities and the resulting policies were often oppressive and unnecessary interventions; sometimes children were even taken away from the disabled parent, who, more often than not, was the mother. In the reaction that set in after some excessive interventions, researchers countered that children can gain from care giving and should have the opportunity to recognize others' needs (Newman 2002). Amy Mullin (2005) argued that child rearing over emphasized the unique needs of the child, ignoring the needs of the caregivers (pp. 178-81). Recently, in Britain, a more reasoned policy has been developed in the social services that emphasizes finding ways to give assistance to a disabled mother so that she can care for her child but get the assistance she needs.

The experience of Julie and her family reflects the complexity and discomfort of the issue of children helping a disabled parent but by no means provides a solution or answer to the question.

Julie: I'm very much 'This is me' I'm in your face! Do you mind?

Julie is 44 and has a degenerative condition (Friedrich's Ataxia). She has two children, 14 and 9, a son and a daughter. Her disability is progressive. When her children were infants and toddlers, despite balance and gait problems, she managed quite well alone with the help of her husband at night. She is now in a wheelchair and more severely impaired and has a helper twice a week who helps prepare food, generally doing meal prep for the week; she also takes Julie's daughter to a dance class.

The family is experiencing a lot of anger, each one for his or her own reasons, and a DSS social worker has been assigned to come three times a week for a year to check up on them and to help them with their problems. One of the issues is whether or not the children are being asked to do too much for Julie and whether the family is, in general, overwhelmed.

Julie managed the care of her babies by herself when the infants were young. She used a car seat to take them up and down the stairs, one step at a time holding onto the railing or she attached "Sarah's Ride"—a belly strap fitting in front—to carry the baby around. Her son started walking at nine months so they put up many baby gates and she put him in a playpen while she was cooking. Her daughter wouldn't stay confined so she used a swing attached to a door frame which worked well. As her balance and gait got worse, Julie had to make some changes, such as getting a new stroller system that made transporting the children easier.

Her husband was helpful, particularly at first, in feeding and bathing and doing some night duty for the infants. He was, of course, not available during the day and as Julie says, "He works a sixty hour week." Friends and family were also supportive.

Julie: When I started using a wheelchair, I got shock and dismay from the public

Julie remembers that she began to experience a different attitude from the outside world's reactions to her when she became a mother. She had been used to "passing" as an able bodied person despite a bad gait, but when she was with the children she was scrutinized more. She remembers one day when she took one of her children to Canobie Lake Park that a security guard approached her because he'd been told that a woman in a yellow shirt looked drunk when getting into her car with a child. She responded, "I'm wearing a yellow shirt, but clearly I'm not drunk."

But, she continues "When I started using a wheelchair, I got shock and dismay from the public." Not until she got known in her own town did she feel at ease. Then she found the police and firemen helpful, even taking her home if her wheelchair broke down. They've recently moved to another town so Julie says she'll have to wait and see how she is received.

Julie: It was no big deal to him, because I was just who I was

In discussing her children's attitude toward her disability, Julie recalls that when her son was about three or four, he asked questions about her disability. "Functional questions, she says, such as "Why can't you do this?" He asked, for instance, why she couldn't give him a really big push on the playground swing like his friend's mother did.

"Because I could pass physically, for him, Julie explains, it wasn't about anything he could see. It was about 'why aren't you doing this?'" When Julie explained to him, "It's because I don't have the balance," he responded, "Oh, OK, no problem." She says, "And you know it was no big deal to him because I was just who I was."

With the other children at school, her son continued to see his mother's disability as nothing unusual. He answered curious questions with "That's just who she is," and then walked away. The school officials, Julie says, "freaked out" and concluded, rightly or wrongly, that he was having problems accepting her disability and they asked her to talk to him more about it. This prompted Julie to act: "I wrote a story and I had a whole bunch of kids his age and older illustrate the story, which was about 'Mommy and my Family.'"

She has used the story for her daughter's classes as well—from preschool to fourth grade. She also talks to the classes about "accepting differences" but her daughter always reminds her to read the story.

Presently, the Department of Social services has become part of the family's lives. Julie places their interventions after an incident when her husband became angry and twisted her wrist. Her daughter was there at the time. Julie describes her memory of a subsequent counseling session with the three of them:

> *The counselor decided that [the incident] was abusive for the children, She mandatorily (sic) reported that my husband and I were neglecting the children. So that's how the Social Services got involved. They've decided that the problem is what you see on the news frequently...stupid stories about kids taking care of their parents. Their fear is that the kids are not getting any of their needs met because they're waiting on me.*

Julie feels she doesn't ask too much of her children. Her husband feels that she does. She says, "I am responsible for the laundry. I am responsible for the household. I am responsible for the meals and generally for the shopping, though my husband took our son shopping for the first time this last weekend." "In general," she says, "he has become more involved, partly, she feels, because of the anticipation of the visits from the DSS."

"I'm very much 'This is me. I'm in your face. I hope you don't mind,'" laughs Julie. She says she has given the social worker a key to the house so she can come at any time. "

Like all pre-teens and teenage children, Julie's son and daughter reflect some of the conflicts around them and have different ways of approaching the issues that the DSS feels needs to be addressed. Each child, says Julie, is different. About her daughter, she says, "I think she actually does a pretty good job of telling me what she wants and what she needs. My son doesn't always do that."

She continues that when she calls her daughter for some help her daughter is really good about saying, "OK. I'm doing this now, and I need a half hour for my work, uninterrupted."

Her son, on the other hand, she says, "will pretend he doesn't hear me. I'll have to call him on his cell phone! Or he'll come and do part of the job and then leave and not come back. He thinks you're going to get distracted about something else. He's no dummy!"

Julie realizes events can come to a crisis and that she and the children can have a confrontation. She had one when her daughter had not picked up her room before an event and was told she couldn't go out. Julie says, "My daughter walked over and kicked me. The idea of it completely destroyed me." Both she and her daughter had a melt down.

Julie also recalls happier events. She describes a more typical day with her children.

> *I met my son downtown in the library and then I bought him a cocoa at Starbucks and then I bribed him into getting a haircut and bought a book for the bribe! And when I got home I sat on the couch with my daughter and we ate apples and caramel sauce and drank hot chocolate and she talked to me about whatever was going on.*

Since Julie's disease is progressive, her needs change as the children grow up. Kate in Chapter One referred to her daughter's independent, even defiant personality, but also to the fact that as an adult, she is more able to understand her mother's needs and even want to participate in helping her solve them. Julie's children, who are preteen or just going into adolescence, are having a difficult time sorting out conflicting needs. Her husband, of course, is also involved. Personalities make a difference, as well. We remember Kate's words about how she feels after many years of fighting and overcoming challenges from her disability and also from her teenage daughter. Now she says, "I feel retired!" Hopefully, Julie will say that some day, too.

2. INDEPENDENCE AND RESPONSIBILITY: DEVELOPING A PARTNERSHIP

Dorothy: I try to partnership with him

Dorothy, who was born with cerebral palsy, has a fourteen year old son. She works full time. Her son wants some independence but he also feels very responsible for his mom, particularly since a divorce. She is very aware that he should not try to take on the role of his father and she says, "That's why I try to partnership with him." They are mutually supportive of one another.

More than most mothers who might worry about asking too much of their children, mothers with disabilities—as Julie or Lily and others have already expressed—fear over-dependency on their children. Dorothy worries about that, too, but seems to be finding a good balance. She speaks of how she has worked it out over the years and how proud she is of her teenager: "Even at his most difficult times, he is truly a blessing."

Dorothy recalls that there were times when she needed to call on her son for help in an emergency. For instance, once she fell on the driveway, slippery with leaves in the fall. She had put her crutch down to get on the curb to the walkway, and the crutch went into an opening in the sewer lid:

> *The way I ended twisting, I actually hurt my shoulder. Thank goodness for my cell phone because it was just he [her son] and I at home. His dad was still with us then but he was working. I had to call Bill from my cell phone and say,*

'Bill, I need you to come out. I've taken a fall.' So he had to come and help me get up.

Dorothy: I have to think outside the box

From her son's infancy, Dorothy has had to be creative and adaptive in caring for him, like so many other disabled mothers. Her family and her husband's family live in other states, so they were not able to be around a lot to help. Tod, her husband (they married after Bill was born), was very good in sharing some of the care, particularly in carrying the baby to the car or up the stairs, and good friends were supportive in the ten weeks Dorothy stayed at home with her new born.

Dorothy said that she found very little adaptive equipment available, such as a crib without a foot release or an adaptable baby carrier. Even her occupational therapist, who paid some home visits, did not have any information, suggesting another gap in healthcare professionals' training. Dorothy spent a lot of time finding a stroller that she could push and which would not tip over. "You have to come up with ways to do things,' she says. You have to think outside the box."

The biggest challenge was keeping Bill by her side and getting him in and out of the car when he was a toddler. She taught him to hold onto her crutches:

> *I would just undo the strap in the car and he would be out so I taught him very early to just hold onto my crutches and at this point he was little enough and he wasn't strong enough to affect my balance. He would stay with me. He just made it that he was helping mommy walk and he knew he had to stay at my speed.*

Dorothy says Bill always wanted to help her even as a toddler. She remembers the day when she was getting ready to take a bath and Bill who was there, came over and just lifted her leg into the bathtub because he had seen his father do that for her. She realized then how observant he had been about her needs and how natural it was for him to help her.

Of course there were times when Bill didn't think of consequences. Dorothy remembers one time in particular when he was about three and they went to Walmart's and he ran away from her:

> *Bill saw a big tower of stacks of mulch on the grass and he ran over and climbed to the top, shouting to me, "Hi mom!" I was so embarrassed and I tried to tell him, "Come on, Bill, get down, "but I was afraid he might fall. I had to get the attention of a store person and then the manager. He was a really nice guy and said 'Don't worry, I will get him.' Bill had a big grin on his face when he came down like he'd made a big accomplishment!*

As he becomes a teenager, Bill remains very protective, Dorothy says. He often asks if she needs any help, but since the divorce, she's made sure he has certain chores but not necessarily all those his father did. "I didn't want him to feel that because his dad wasn't there that he had to pickup and assume that role because that wasn't his role; his role is he's my son."

Dorothy has needed more help since she recently injured herself, so she decided to hire a PCA to do the laundry, which is downstairs in the basement, and to do vacuuming and cleaning. Bill does the trash, the raking and the shoveling. The grocery shopping, she says, has become a family activity that they do together. "When I take him shopping I always spend more money with him but it's important that he is part of it and has input! I don't want him to grow up and feel like, oh man, my mom made me do so much! That's why I try to partnership so much with him!"

Keeping open communications is not always easy with a teenager, but Dorothy has been able to talk to her son about her disability of cerebral palsy and how it can affect people very differently. That has been information that Bill has experienced personally because he has a friend in Boy Scouts, a boy who has CP and has difficulty speaking and is pretty much non verbal. "Bill has kind of befriended him," Dorothy says, "He can talk to him but he uses some sign language so that he can understand what the boy is trying to tell him. He's got a lot of awareness and sensitivity in that way."

Dorothy has always been very open to others about her disability, particularly at Bill's schools—from nursery school to high school where he is now a freshman. She answers questions about her crutches and why she needs them and about her particular disability. She thinks it's important to educate children about disabilities, "I get approached a lot and sometimes a parent will just pull a child away, saying 'don't ask' and the kid feels like they did something wrong. I'm very open and comfortable about talking about it."

Most of the mothers interviewed have been very active in school activities and have overcome what might be some shyness in participating as a person with a disability. Dorothy has not been shy and has attended teacher conferences and school events and her son's sports activities without hesitation. She does remember, however, some difficult moments, Once in one of Bill's fourth grade presentations, she was a little late and hurried in the door onto a slippery floor and fell. Bill was up on stage, waiting to do his piece, and saw her come in:

> *You could see the fear go across his face. The teacher didn't know what to do, but there were a couple of Dads there and they got me up. Bill started to cry and, of course, when I saw that, I started to fill up, too. He still remembers that. He's in ninth grade now, but he still remembers that day in fourth grade when I went flying into his classroom!*

Dorothy recalls the moment with some embarrassment but also with humor. Dorothy is not sure whether Bill was mostly frightened or whether he was also embarrassed. "I think he might have been feeling embarrassed, too," she says.

Dorothy knows that Bill as a teenager is sometimes embarrassed, not because of her disability, but just because she's his mom. He tells her she cheers too loudly at his games and when she picks him up after school, he doesn't want to wait for her where the girls are playing softball: "Mom," he says, "I don't want to be hanging around watching the girls softball team. Come on, you need to move!"

Bill is a typical teenager in other ways, as well. He'll put off doing a chore if he is in the middle of a video or computer game. And Dorothy says, "Like any teenager, you get the attitude. Sometimes, his dad and I are the dumbest people on the earth. Since he became fourteen, we've become stupid!"

If he has issues, Dorothy says, they are mostly teenage issues. After she and Tod separated and went through a difficult divorce, she sent Bill to a counselor, but he hasn't had serious problems. "He is not acting out, he's not getting into trouble at school, he's not skipping school. In fact, he's made honor roll the first two marking periods. He's very motivated in school."

Dorothy feels that showing how she feels about herself has helped her son relate to her disability as he grows and develops:

> *I think the fact that I am very comfortable with who I am has taught him that the way I am is okay. I learned to accept the way I am and do things and get things done and that's the one thing that I really try to impart to him. He has a reading disability at school but he can figure out ways he can compensate for that because he excels in other areas. I feel that I had a responsibility to him to be a good role model and part of that is not giving* up.

Bill does excel in other areas and already has a direction about where he wants to go. He is in an engineering technology academy at school and works on robotics, which is his passion. His team is very competitive and they are working on a robotic arm. They are going to Connecticut and to Dallas, Texas, to compete. Bill is already seeking out some part-time jobs to earn money to pay for part of the trip.

Bill is also thinking of ways his interest and talents in engineering can help his mother. He is planning an adaptive device that can help her get into a car like an SUV, where she could see more of the road. He says, "Mom, I'm going to develop something that is going to lift you up and swivel you into the car seat." As Dorothy says, "He thinks that way, his mind thinks that way, which is great!"

Dorothy is grateful that her son has made a good transition into high school and into his teenage years. "He towers over me now," she says, "and he is developing into a really great young adult." Her disability and becoming a single mom—though Bill still has his dad in his life—have been challenging for both of them but, she feels that those challenges have made Bill more caring and responsible and sensitive to others.

3. CREATING COMMUNITY AND FAMILY

Mothers with disabilities do at times feel frustrated and sometimes guilty about the tasks they cannot perform. But all the women interviewed here felt they had more than made up for their limitations in their roles as mothers. A common theme for all these women was the importance of creating an environment for their families where reaching out to others and respecting their needs was important.

Two mothers, Donna and Janice, created a larger community for their families in which diversity was an accepted part of their lives. Another mother, Bernice, describes being raised in the projects, primarily an African American community, that took care of each other. Mothers were part of a "women centered network" as Patricia Hill Collins would call it (122). This extended family was there for Bernice's daughter as well.

Donna and Janice created their own communities that gave their families a wider perspective of the world.

Donna, born in 1953, had polio as a child. She has created a sense of community that combines her personal and professional life. She lives in co-housing with another family and her two daughters and adopted son and a boy for whom she is a guardian. The two boys are from the school where she is a swimming coach and Aquatics Director and is called "the mom" of her team. Donna was mobile for years, discarding crutches and braces after some experimental orthopedic operations. Now she uses crutches occasionally and has a wheelchair to use when needed.

Donna: Family takes care of family

Donna brought up her children in the context of community, expanding the definition of what makes a family.

After her divorce, she set up co-housing in 1996 with her best friend, who is able bodied. They bought a mansion and divided it into four apartments, two of which they rent. The families have grown up together. "It's an extended family," she says, and by co-parenting when needed, their children could always remain at home. The principle of sharing responsibilities and space became natural. Donna explains: "All the kids were integrated as a family. It was the idea that if one of us wanted to go on a vacation or on a job, the kids wouldn't have to go some place else." They would be in their home.

Donna has also created community in her professional life as a swimming coach and aquatics director in a private school, She thinks of her students—who are able bodied—as family.

She says, "I'm the mom of the school. We have 280 kids. They're all boys and I'm their mom!" And in fact, Matthew, for whom she is a guardian, came to live with her from the school because his parents live far away in St Lucia. "He just needed somebody and my home was becoming his home anyway. His parents were really happy that there was someone that could legally take care of him."

Her own adopted son goes to the school and has joined the swim team. Donna says, "Family takes care of family" and it is clear that for her "family" is inclusive.

In discussing her role as a mother with a disability, Donna names the evening meal as one of the most important moments in bringing her family together: "I may not be able to bring the groceries in, but I can put them away and make the food. Just plain sitting down and eating the meal with the kids. That's probably the most important part."

Her children have always shared responsibilities and have done household tasks though Donna says she needed very little help in housework or even in child care. In the last few years she is experiencing symptoms of post polio syndrome and needs more assistance, "My muscles are getting weaker," she says, and "They [the children] have to do more carrying for me."

Donna recalls when her eighteen year old daughter gave a workshop at her school on what's it's like to have a mother with a disability. Her daughter said, "The biggest drawback I have is that I have to carry everything for her." That, she said, was a drawback, but she added that the "perks much outweigh the drawbacks and include going to Disneyland and getting to stand first in line because people with disabilities get in first!"

Donna emphasizes, as many of these mothers have, that she did not want her children to feel overburdened because of her disability,

> *I did try to make sure that my kids didn't have too many tasks or responsibilities because of my disability. They don't have to take care of me. If I can take care of myself, I am perfectly able to take care of them. If they needed somebody to defend them, whether it was physically or not, I was there to do it.*

Donna: Each one of them has a different relationship

In raising her teenagers, Donna is very perceptive about the different ways her children relate to her and to her disability. "Each one of them has a different relationship," she says. She speaks of Jenny, her oldest, who is 28, and lives nearby and now understands her mother's needs the best.

Jenny is the oldest and she was the most difficult. She was my wild child. We had a poor relationship in her teens. She actually left home when she was sixteen. She was ten when we were going through the divorce and she was angry with her father for a long time. Now she's a great person and she has that intuition. She knows when I need help and knows that I'm suffering more than I used to.

Jenny's anger, now transformed into empathy and understanding, was not, Donna believes, experienced by her younger sister, Stacey, who Donna says "knows me the most and can even joke about my disability—sometimes too much!" When Stacey said in her workshop at school "I have to carry everything," she was not angry, says Donna, but just stating facts and she really felt the perks of growing up with her mother outweighed the drawbacks. Donna remembers the times Stacey, at five or six, accompanied her mother to her Special Ed swimming classes and learned how to talk to and help autistic children: "She looks back on it now as one of the perks. How many five or six year olds can go and talk to kids that are autistic that can't talk? To learn how to do that, and learn that they're real people?"

Matthew, her adopted son and the youngest, came to the family at ten and was accustomed to being a caretaker of his alcoholic mother. His grandmother was Donna's mother's best friend and because of a very dysfunctional family, his grandmother tried to adopt him but was unable physically to do it because of progressive ms. So Donna stepped in. She was uncertain at first if she could manage, but Stacey, then a sophomore in high school, urged her to go ahead. Donna says, "One day it just came to me. I said, 'Wait a minute. There's no decision here.' And that just released the burden on me. And it has worked out."

At first, Matthew was shocked if Stacey joked about her mother's disability. He still felt like a caretaker. "Now, he's learning when he needs to take care and when he doesn't. And he's getting better about feeling that he doesn't always need to protect me."

The other Matthew [same name]—for whom she is legal guardian—is more laidback, Donna says, probably because he is less connected. He doesn't offer help but is glad to help if asked. Donna thinks he is becoming more intuitive, however, about when he should offer assistance and when it is appropriate.

Donna: I wasn't honoring my disability

Donna's independence and take charge abilities started in her childhood when her family expected her to do anything she chose to do despite her disability. They provided her with excellent medical care and let her be responsible for how she handled her disability.

Donna says that looking back now "I didn't really think of myself as disabled. She adds, "And to a point, it was good, but then when I got to my twenties and thirties, it was more that I wasn't honoring my disability. It was more of a denial."

Donna finished college, did two years of graduate school and married. Her first daughter was born in 1983. Donna says, "I never had two thoughts about being a good parent and had always wanted to have children." Her pregnancies and births were uneventful and she has good things to say about her medical care then. She feels less positive about her doctors now, finding them less helpful as she experiences symptoms of post polio syndrome and realizes she has to acknowledge her physical limitations more.

Despite the fact that she lived many years ignoring her disability, Donna now recalls her sense of frustration when she was not able to achieve her ambition as an athlete because of her disability.

Donna: Athleticism was always in my heart

I was always told because I was disabled, I couldn't be an athlete. I think it's been more of a struggle than being a parent. But I kept trying and said, 'I'm going to figure out a way to do this. What sport can I participate in that I can be pretty close to an even level?' And it was swimming.

Like many polio patients, Donna was given aqua therapy—even at nine months—so swimming became part of her life: "I don't remember learning how to swim. I've always been able to swim." Though she achieved great skill in the sport, Donna was not allowed to compete with able bodied swimmers. And yet she was denied taking part in Paralympics or Special Olympics because she was almost at an even level of skill.

Becoming a swimming coach and the Aquatics director at her school has given Donna much satisfaction in achieving her goal in athletics. She's coached her teams to the National level and her teams in swimming, diving, and water polo have competed with high school teams and have won their meets. And yet at times Donna still experiences discrimination when she goes to other schools and she is not recognized as the coach. She recalls an incident at one college where she took a team. She asked for the pool deck and despite wearing her jacket that says Coach, she was repeatedly sent to the watching galley until she finally just followed the swimmers into the deck.

Recently Donna has become more active in disability related activities. She plays indoor wheelchair soccer with a team and she coaches Junior Paralympics and has taken them to Australia and other places. When she was with the teams—there were also track and basketball teams—she realized it was the first time she was not in the minority.

> *I had never been in an environment where I was not a minority. Here I was in the majority and realized how empowering it was. There were only two disabled coaches. The others were able bodied. I could see them [the able bodied] trying to assert their power over the kids using their able bodiedness. And also assert their power over me. It was really interesting to see. One coach was really irked because the kids listened to me more.*

On the same trip, Donna says she experienced the limitations of our ability to identify with another minority group. She was with a majority of young people with disabilities and she realized that it's impossible to know how it feels to be disabled unless you *are* disabled. She says "Unless you're disabled, you don't know how it really feels and you respect that. It's like you can't know how it feels to be black. "She felt the able bodied coaches could not fully identify with the disabled swimmers and were perhaps unconscious of trying to use their able bodied status to dominate and control.

Donna's philosophy of teaching and mentoring her students and her own children involves an important principle of cooperation.

First, she says, I tell the kids that "I can't" are not two words in my vocabulary. They don't look at me and say 'I can't do that. They say 'I'm having a hard time. I may need help. I don't understand. Explain it to me more' And I say 'Never be afraid to ask for help."

And secondly, she urges her students to help each other and be interactive. Growing from her awareness that there are things she teaches, like competitive diving, that she can't actually do herself, Donna emphasizes the importance of depending on each others' knowledge and skill. She'll say to a student, "Why don't you tell this kid who can't do this move what it *feels* like to do it."

At the heart of Donna's philosophy of creating community, mentoring her students and being a mother with a disability to her children, is a belief that we are all interconnected and can help one another even if we cannot exactly be in the other person's shoes. Support and self-responsibility create community.

Janice: I asked my children's permission and they agreed

Janice, who has a spinal cord injury and uses a wheelchair, has created a diverse community—her own daughter and two adopted mixed race brothers. In 1998, Janice married an African American man who has been incarcerated since 1987 for a crime he did not commit. She says she asked her children's permission to marry him and they agreed. They have taken him into their family and she visits him regularly.

Janice tells a story about the challenges of disability, motherhood, adoption, and race.

At 27, Janice was riding on the back of a motorcycle and was struck by a car. She was paralyzed from the chest down and spent seven months in the hospital—one month on a respirator. She had a seven year old daughter at the time and had been recently divorced.

Janice left home at sixteen because of an abusive father. She says her mother was fearful of everything and could not even drive a car for years, though she does now and comes to see the grandchildren. Janice has always been very independent and managed everything on her own, including caring for her children. Her brother and particularly her sister, Shirley, have been supportive and caring. She stayed with her brother for a month after she left the hospital until she found an apartment and Shirley has helped her a lot. "In fact," says, Janice, "she hovers over me a bit too much at times!"

Continuing to take care of her daughter after the accident was not too difficult. Her daughter was easy to discipline and did not try to run off as her adopted sons did later on. I asked Janice about her decision to adopt a child, and eventually another. The adoption would be the first time Janice would take care of a baby as a disabled mother.

Janice: I didn't think I could raise a child from a wheelchair

Janice explains that she wanted more children but didn't think she could raise a child from a wheelchair. Then her niece became pregnant and was rejected by her mother. Janice took her in and kept her for two years, doing much of the baby care. She realized she could do it so in 1988 she adopted a five-day-old mixed race boy. Three years later, she adopted his biological brother. Her daughter was fourteen at the time and said she would love to have a baby brother.

The adoption process, Janice says, was very rigorous. She was evaluated and was given a stringent home study to see how she would make adaptations to care for the infant. When the second child came, she had two in diapers (the second son had medical problems). She often relied on a buzzer system connected to her daughter's bedroom so she could call her to come and help at night. Years later, her daughter's husband told Janice that her daughter had hated the buzzer, but she was helpful, nevertheless, and remains close to her mother now with a child of her own.

Janice's two boys were harder to discipline than her daughter and she recalls that they wouldn't sit in the corner for "time out" so she had to shut them in their rooms and sit outside the door! They both live at home now as teenagers and one of them goes to college. Janice still drives both of them around because she is reluctant to let the older one get a license just yet.

Janice: My children never talk about my disability

I asked Janice whether her children have talked to her about her disability and she says when asked about it, they say it's nothing to them. They're used to it! Once when she asked them if they wished they had an able bodied mother, they said, "No, we're happy."

The general public and even some neighbors have not been as supportive to Janice as a disabled mother, however. She found that people usually stared at her in a wheelchair when she had the two young boys with her and one older woman actually said, "How can you take care of little kids in a wheelchair?"

Janice is tolerant, however, and feels that older people may associate persons in wheelchairs with invalids and not with fully competent adults. As for the children who stare, she knows they are curious and interested and might sometimes ask if they can sit in the chair.

Two different neighbors called the Social Services and complained of child abuse or endangerment because Janice had a swimming pool. On each occasion, a social worker came to the house and checked out the pool—the fence and gate, which self-locks—and concluded that everything was fine and that the children looked good. One of them, Janice recalls, even said to her, "You have to be very good at what you do or crazy to adopt two kids!"

Nevertheless, says Janice "I always had that fear that the boys might be taken away from me." She actually didn't take them out much when they were young and rambunctious, she says.

Janice has dealt with many negative attitudes toward herself as a mother. She names the reasons: first of all, she is a disabled mother and then she had the nerve to adopt two more children and they were boys of mixed race. She is annoyed when people ask her "Is that your own child?" She answers curtly, "Yes, it is *my* child!"

As for the racial issue, Janice says she has always lived with racial prejudice because she grew up with African American friends and often had black boy friends. In the seventies, she was used to getting hostile looks when she was with a black man. Her children are quite light skinned and look Hispanic. She is aware of racial attitudes toward them though they seem unaware of it. She has spoken to them about racism in general but she's not sure how much they understand.

One thing Janice is sure about her children. They have learned a lot from living in a family that is diverse and a little different from "the norm." They are "more sensitized to people and have learned to help others," says Janice, and "They are more independent than other children their age."

Her children approve of her husband, but he has been sentenced to 25 to 50 years and at present has little hope of getting out. They have tried the Innocence Project but there is no material evidence to work with for his appeal; he continues to be part of their life. Janice has developed her talents as an artist, working in pastels. She has a studio in her home and has also exhibited her work.

As mothers with disabilities, Donna and Janice have worked hard to make family inclusive. Each builds a community that is not only equally comfortable with the able bodied and disabled world, but also expands the vision of family to include more diversity.

Bernice: We lived in the projects. Everybody was friends and we did things for each other. It was a community

Bernice, born in 1952, contracted polio at seventeen months. She was in an iron lung and now uses a leg brace and an electric wheel chair. She has a daughter, 2 grandsons and 1 granddaughter.

Bernice has always experienced the warmth and care of a community of family and friends. She has extended that to her own daughter and grandchildren. When she contracted polio as a toddler, her family took it in stride. She says her older sister cared for her a lot. "She used to take me around and she said she always wanted to carry me wherever she went. She said I was kind of like her little baby doll."

Bernice also had three older brothers who, she says, "protected me" so she felt completely safe and at home in the projects in a predominantly African American community in Roxbury where members of her family had lived for over forty years. So it is not surprising that she did not want to go to a special needs school instead of the local public school which her family and friends attended. Her mother was fearful of how she would manage at public school but Bernice felt differently.

She says, "I felt that I could survive and play out with my friends and family in the project, just running up and down the stairs and climbing the fences. And if you could see somebody climb the fence who can't use her arms to hold on, that's a pretty strange sight but I did it."

Bernice was sent to a special needs school, then called "The Industrial School for Crippled Children" in Boston, now called the Cotting School in Lexington. She says "I hated it because of its name." And she hated the fact that she was sent on a bus that was "like the crippled school bus." She had been used to being treated like any other kid in her neighborhood and not as someone segregated by a disability.

Bernice admits in retrospect that the education at the school was good, but she says "I wanted to go to public school so bad. " So she made a plan. She would get herself expelled.

I knew that if we got caught smoking in the school, we would be kicked out. So I took a cigarette to school one day, went into the ladies room, which I think

was really close to the office, and I told one of my school mates to light it. She
was scared to death and she lit it and she left very quickly. And I sat there and
I puffed and puffed until they could smell smoke out in the hall and they came
in and they caught me smoking. And they kicked me out of the school and I was
so happy!

After she was expelled, Bernice went to the James T. Timilty Junior High School where her sister and her three brothers had gone and where her friends were and she felt "one of the gang" again.

After she finished high school, Bernice attended the University of Massachusetts at Amherst but she found the campus too spread out for her to negotiate. "I wasn't the advocate that I should have been at the time," she says. She transferred to University of Massachusetts, Boston, and received a B.A. and a Master's degree with a concentration in Rehabilitation Counseling. At present she is a Rehab counselor at the Massachusetts Rehabilitation Commission; she takes The Ride to work and sometimes public transportation, using her electric wheelchair. She finds access to transportation improving, but she says it's "as good as it is until it gets better!"

Bernice had her daughter when she was twenty-five while she was in college. She had a relationship with a man and decided she wanted a child. She says, "This wasn't an accidental pregnancy. I had met this person. I liked him and I said, 'I want to have a child by him'. We stayed together for a while after the birth and we were friends afterwards." He died when her daughter was four.

Bernice remembers her experience with doctors and the hospital as a good one when she was pregnant and gave birth. This was in direct contrast to her very bad memories of doctors when she was a child and had to spend a lot of time in a hospital for children run by nuns. Like Martha in Part One, she found the medical profession insensitive, but more than that, she found them abusive:

I always felt the doctors were in a way using me. I felt that I was being
paraded around and showed off as if I were a piece of meat or something. And
when I was in the hospital, I felt some of the nuns and some of the medical
professionals were really abusive.

Bernice: I was going to be the boss of my body

Bernice says she has many stories to tell of those times, including memories of being put out on a closed in porch by herself at night because she wet the bed. These memories, she says, helped her decide when she was eighteen that she was "going to be the boss of my body." She says, "If I needed any kind of surgery or medication or whatever, I was going to be in charge. And that's what I did pretty much, so that's what I did."

Shelly was born just before Mother's Day and Bernice was excited that it was her first Mother's day being a mother. She was awake during the delivery and "saw my little baby when they took her out."

It takes a village....

Although Bernice had her own apartment when her daughter was born, she stayed with her mother for a couple of months after the birth. The father would come and help her out, too. Friends and family were all available. She remembers that even a young boy from the apartment upstairs would come down and sterilize the bottles for her when needed.

> *Like I said, we lived in the projects for over forty years, so we knew everybody. We still do. And so everybody was friends and we did things for each other. It was a community and still is. I still keep in touch with my friends.*

Like the other disabled mothers, Bernice made adaptations in caring for her daughter. Her aunt made her a sling in which she carried the baby, but not the usual way. " I would lay her in the sling and close it up and carry her around in my mouth because I can't use my left arm at all and my right arm has been kind of getting worse as we speak."

Bernice remembers that at times it was a little rough but she really had all the support she needed.

> *I've got so many sisters, nieces… and you know someone would do my hair for me all the time and buy everything I needed. I loved going shopping which I did by myself or with someone else if I needed to.*

Her daughter, Shelly, grew up as part of the community and extended family. If Bernice needed assistance, someone was always there. However, she did rely on her daughter to do things for her. "She used to help me do a lot of stuff. She used to do all kinds of things. She helped in the house, helped me get dressed…before I knew about Personal Care Assistants." Bernice now uses PCAs to help her with her tasks of daily living.

Shelly was protective of her mother and was quick to react if anyone made a remark about her. Bernice recalls an incident:

> *She told me that one time when I had gone with her to the bus stop, one of the kids made a comment about me and she beat him up. When she told me, I said 'Oh, cool!' And they never said anything again about me!*

I asked Bernice if she and her daughter talked about her disability and she recalled that although Shelly took her mother's disability for granted, she was curious. "She used to ask me why I did things the way I did. We used to always color and I would color with my foot so she thought that was real cool and I still do that."

Like any teenager, Shelly also acted out. Bernice says, "She was a real nut. She was crazy. She was a good nut. She would get angry with me about different things but it wasn't about my disability. She would get angry about not getting her way or not getting something she wanted, the regular kid stuff."

Later in our interview, Bernice spoke again about her daughter's reaction to having been her mother's caretaker at times. "I'm sure she probably feels guilty knowing that I needed her to do things for me and sometimes her not wanting to."

Bernice also spoke of her own pain and guilt for not being able to do things for her daughter:

> *You want to be able to do all of the physical things that other moms can do, and when you can't it's a real bitch. You know, I couldn't pick her up and put her in the tub when I wanted to. And I couldn't do her hair myself. I think a mother and a daughter get a certain bond when they do things together. Especially with African Americans. I remember when my mother used to do my hair and my sister used to do my hair and I would sit there and we would talk, you know. I feel like I may have missed out and that she didn't get from me things I wanted to give her.*

In her advice to other disabled women who are thinking of becoming a parent, Bernice emphasizes, "Don't use your children for the things you can get services for." Of course, she was not aware that she probably could have had help with PCAs after her daughter was born.

Bernice reflected on what she was able to pass on to her daughter:

> *I think if anything I hope she learned that I am a determined person. I'm really determined. I've always been. When I was younger my grandmother—that's what she called me. She called me "Determined." No matter what the circumstances were, I was going to complete, or get or do whatever it was that I wanted or needed. I didn't care if it took me two or three years longer, I was going to do it*

Bernice and her daughter are still part of a community and an extended family. Shelly has three children: a son 15, one 13 and a daughter 10. She lives nearby and during our interview, one or more of her grandchildren were in and out of the apartment. I remarked on how much she must enjoy her grand children.

She said, "Yeah, I do. I enjoy them and sometimes I enjoy them so much I have to tell them to stay away from me! I'm involved with my family a lot. It is so much fun!"

4. FROM THE CHILD'S PERSPECTIVE

Children cannot always articulate their feelings and attitudes about growing up with a disabled mother. My children, when asked, didn't have much to say until my youngest daughter wrote about it on her website, resulting in a dialogue among us.

Many of the women in this book said they were able to talk about and explain to their children their disability—what it was and how it developed. And in the case of the child being disabled as well, such as Molly's son with HSP or Ellen's son with ROB, the conversation was on-going and mutually important.

Other women mentioned reactions their children had to their disability. Kate spoke of her daughter, Sarah's anger growing up with a disabled mother and Bernice said her daughter "acted out" as a teenager, partly in response to her relationship to her mother's disability. We remember the tensions in Julie's family, including her husband's disagreement about how much she should ask her children to take on tasks for her.

However, we do not have these women's stories actually told from their children's point of view.

There are not many books written by children growing up with disabled parents. There are some which stand out for their eloquence and insight: Kathryn Black's *In the Shadow of Polio: A Personal and Social History* (1996) is an account of the personal struggle and tragedy of her mother's death from polio placed in the social history of the time. Lennard J. Davis' *My Sense of Silence: Memoirs of a Childhood with Deafness* (2000) traces his emotional struggle with anger growing up in an immigrant family as interpreter for his deaf parents and ends with his enlightenment and participation in deaf culture and in the disability movement as a professor.

The last interview in this book is with a young woman, a student, who worked with me in a student scholar program at Brandeis University's Women's Studies Research Center. When she applied to work in my project as a student assistant, she wrote that she was drawn to the subject of mothers with disabilities because of her own experience of growing up with a mother who has multiple sclerosis. She explained that, as she approached college graduation, she realized she wanted to know more about disabilities and how her mother's disability had affected her life. "My mother's illness has in one way or another affected much of my life but it has never directly impacted the course of my academic study. I have lived with the daily influence that my mother's multiple sclerosis has had on my life very much in a degree of isolation. I never knew other disabled mothers; I never interacted with other children of disabled parents."

Sarah became much involved in the research on mothers with disabilities and in reading the transcripts of interviews and material in my project. Her insights, as a child of a mother with a disability, were invaluable. Her interview added a fresh perspective, revealing the conflicting emotions of pain and joy and of alienation and commitment.

Sarah: I felt very unsafe

Sarah Linet was born in 1988 and graduated from Brandeis University in 2010.When Sarah was four, her mother was hospitalized for the first time because of multiple sclerosis. Sarah remembers the hospitalization but she was unaware of why her mother was ill. During the next years her mother began to have difficulty in walking and gradually retired from her practice as a pediatrician. The family moved to another town because their house had a flight of stairs.

Sarah remembers the first day at her new school. Her mother had walked her in and then left. The children, whom Sarah didn't know, gathered around her and asked, "What's wrong with your mother? Why does she limp? What's wrong with her foot?"

Sarah was traumatized. She had never before felt her family was "different." "I felt very unsafe," Sarah says, and "I ran away from my teacher." She was sent to the school psychologist who called home and told her mother Sarah needed therapy before she could return to school. Her mother was outraged and told them she was a respected pediatrician and that there was nothing wrong with her daughter. Sarah was sent back to school the next day and nothing more was said of it.

As her mother's mobility decreased—she moved to crutches and a wheelchair—Sarah and her sister took on more of the care giving though her father, she says, was the primary care giver. A lawyer, he works at home in his own office, and can be available. They have gradually added personal care attendants for her mother over time, but during Sarah's teenage years, she and her sister took on a lot of tasks. Sarah says at eleven, she started cooking dinners, which she loved to do, particularly for Thanksgiving and Jewish holidays. Cooking often included planning and shopping as well. When her mother was still driving she would take them to the grocery store and Sarah and her sister would go in and shop for the food.

The tasks divided rather naturally between the two sisters. Her sister didn't like to cook so she did more of the personal care. But Sarah feels that they differ quite sharply in how their mother's disability affects them. She feels that she struggles more than her sister with her mother's Illness. "My sister 'compartmentalizes' and feels that her mother's illness has affected "just about nothing' in her life." Sarah, on the other hand, feels that the illness has affected "every part of our lives."

Sarah: I was a parent to her

Sarah recalls that, at times, she felt like a parent to her mother but at the same time she felt that her mother was invincible and "that nothing would ever happen to her." So when her mother was suddenly hospitalized with a high fever, when Sarah was in twelfth grade, she and her family were over-whelmed. At first, the doctors could not make a diagnosis and they all feared cancer. Her mother was kept in the hospital for two weeks and the family and many relatives took over the waiting room, bringing food and taking turns visiting. Her father stayed in the hospital most nights.

Sarah's reaction to this trauma, she feels, was denial and she kept saying to her mother "You'll be fine." Finally when the doctors found the cause in a reaction to an experimental drug for her MS, her mother recovered and went home. But the episode remained vivid in Sarah's memory. It changed her relationship with her peers at school. She found her friends' problems seemed trivial, even stupid, and she couldn't share her feelings with them. More than ever, she was frightened at the thought of leaving home for college and not being there for her mother. She chose a college (among the ones where she was accepted) that was the nearest to where they lived—they had recently moved to Maine from Massachusetts. In the summer of her freshman year she took a job in Rhode Island, and when she heard that her mother had broken her knee, for the first time Sarah had to say "I can't come home."

Despite the increasingly deteriorating nature of her MS, her mother remains the center of the family and her spirit drives them all. Among the many treasured memories of good times with her mother, Sarah recalls her sister's graduation from college (before her own), when for two days her mother didn't miss a thing in the celebrations. And an earlier memory in the summer before seventh grade when the family spent a month in Israel. Her mother was in a wheelchair but could still walk. They had a lovely holiday and shared a Passover celebration with relatives.

In her interview, Sarah analyzed the affect of her mother's disability on her life, identifying the three important moments when she was changed by becoming more aware of her mother's disability.

The first was the time she, at four years, old, walked into her new school with her mother and was confronted with questions by the other children. Sarah describes feeling "unsafe." She had never been singled out as having a mother with a disability and probably had not even noticed that her mother was "different.

The second episode was in Sarah's twelfth grade year when her mother was very ill and in the hospital with no specific diagnosis. Sarah admits she was in complete denial and insisted that her mother was invincible. This experience changed Sarah's relationship to her peers in school. Life was too serious for teenage concerns. Sarah worried that her mother was not safe and this fear affected her plans for going away to college.

The third episode was in the summer of her freshman year at college when she had a job in Rhode Island and her mother broke her knee. Sarah realized she could not just leave her job and go home to help her mother. The separation from her role as care taker and her obligation to her own life had begun.

The conflicts and stages of her teenage and young adult years have been heightened and shaped by Sarah's relationship to her mother's disability. She comes out of them with much wisdom. She called her experience of finding out about other mothers and families with disabilities "transformative" for her. She expresses her feelings about her mother and her family eloquently in the following essay.

Sarah: Has her [mother's] disability brought us pain? Yes, it has. But it has also brought us closer than any other family I know. Even when MS made her weak, it made us strong.

LESSONS LEARNED BY SARAH LINET

My mother is the strongest woman that I know. Not because of her disability and the way she has dealt with the setbacks in her life; not even in spite of her disability. She is strong because she has balanced a career and a family. Because she has lived her life on her own terms. Because she is smart, strong, funny, brave and incredibly wise. Because she has a quick tongue and a strong sense of herself. She is strong because she knows exactly how much seltzer water to put in matzah balls (a family secret) and exactly what to do to mend a pulled muscle or a broken heart. She is strong because she is my mother, my sister's mother, my father's wife and she still knows how to be herself.

My mother tells a story about talking to a former neighbor of ours. They were discussing the discrimination he felt his own daughters would face as women in the professional world. He said, "Aren't you worried that your daughters won't succeed in math and science? That they will feel limited in what they can do?" At the time my sister (all of three years old) thought that only women were allowed to be doctors, my mother and the majority of her female friends being doctors themselves. Women doctors were all that my sister had ever known. My mother told our neighbor that he was a buffoon (her words, not mine), that her daughters could do anything, could succeed in any field that they wanted to and that they would know it.

At the time my mother was not only a mother of two young children, she was also a respected and revered pediatrician, active in our synagogue, and on the board of the United Way in our town. She was super-woman, a product of the post-feminist generation. She had wanted to be a doctor since she was three years old, almost as long as she wanted to be a mother. My parents saw parenthood as the ultimate prize. My mother worked with children professionally and could not wait to have her own. My father is a lawyer whose love of kids has been expressed in how he spent (and spends) his time outside of the office. When he met my mother he was a "big brother" to a boy in Miami and he worked his way through law school in part by babysitting for a judge's children.

My parents had a whirlwind love affair, the stuff of romantic novels and pipedreams. I truly believe that their love is the once in a lifetime fairytale type of relationship of which some people can only dream. They were young and sure and ready and within eight weeks of meeting each other at a wedding they were engaged. Within two years they had my sister and moved back to Boston. Two years (and a house in the suburbs later), they had me. I do not mean to brag, but it truly was the beautiful family they had always imagined. Things had not always been easy but they always had each other, and then us.

When I was three or four years old the dream and our lives changed forever. My mother was diagnosed with multiple sclerosis. The disease has taken a fairly extreme course. MS has taken so much from my mother. It took the career she had always loved and spent her whole life working toward. It took her final degree (she was eight tenths through her MBA when she was forced to retire and end her studies). It took her independence. It took her ability to walk. It took her ability to feed herself, to brush her own hair, to get herself dressed. But it never once took her ability to be a mother. MS never took her ability to love my father or to take care of us.

Has her disease hurt us—her family; hurt me and my sister—her daughters; and hurt all of the people who love her? Yes, it has hurt us. Sometimes the pain of what she has lost hurts me so much that I struggle to breathe. I live in almost constant, sometimes paralyzing fear of what she will lose next. Her disease has forced me and my sister to grow up sooner and faster than we would have otherwise, and to be brave and strong in ways that maybe children shouldn't be. It gave us increased responsibility around our house, and it has made it harder for us to leave. We have wrestled with the dual desires to live our own lives—to be free, independent and strong women capable (as our mother always knew we would be) of running the world, of changing the world, of being extraordinary—and the desire to stay home. To be with my mother. To help her and make her smile and take care of her and protect her from all of the things she has been through, protect her from a life that is not the one she chose and the pain that inevitably goes with that.

Unlike many of the women in this book, my mother was not disabled when she became a mother. I do not know if she would have had children had she known what course her life would take. I would never claim to guess or question or assume anything about her choices. What I do know is that my sister and I bring her tremendous joy. She wouldn't trade us for anything in this world and I would never trade any of them. I have learned more from my parents and sister than I have from anyone else in this world. Have her disability and her disease brought us pain? Yes, they have. But they also brought us closer together then any other family I know. Even when MS made her weak, it made us strong. I cannot imagine a life without her. She gave me life and she is my heart.

LESSONS TO SHARE

For Mothers with Disabilities

Children may feel guilty about not doing enough to help a disabled mother. The mother may in turn feel guilty about asking too much from her child.

It is not unusual for children to feel anger about a mother's disability; perhaps feeling that they should not express their own problems with a mother "so brave" or perhaps feeling that they are asked to do too much for their mother.

Discussing these issues with your child or with a counselor can be helpful.

Some mothers feel they can develop a partnership with their child where they help each other.

Recognize that each child in your family has a different reaction to your disability.

Let older children explain your disability to their friends in their own way.

Create a community or an environment where your children become sensitive to the needs of others and more aware that we live in a world that is interconnected.

For Counselors and Social Workers

A recent study of parents with disabilities (sixty-two percent of them mothers) and their teenagers concludes that parents with disabilities raising teens are more like than unlike parents without disabilities.

Recent studies have argued that child rearing policies have often over emphasized the needs of the child of a disabled mother and ignored her needs, such as having assistance to help her in care giving.

Chapter Five

What Mothers with Disabilities Know

The stories of these women demonstrate the challenges they face as mothers and the strategies for success they use throughout the stages of mothering. As mothers with disabilities, they defy the stereotypes society imposes on them, whether it is seeing them as imperfect women or possible biological risks as reproducers or classifying them as care receivers who therefore cannot be caregivers for their children.

These women not only defy negative stereotypes, they believe they have something unique to offer as mothers. Ellen, who lives with her own disability and that of her son, feels that disabled women "are able to discuss things that other people don't understand" and she adds, "There's a lot that I bring to the table in my relationship with my husband and my children that I don't think other parents have." Lily echoes this belief that having a disability gives you extra insight: "We have so much to give to other people. That's if they're willing to listen and not just judge outside appearances." Many of the women felt their children learned valuable lessons in living with a disabled mother. Lorrie, for instance, says of her daughter, "She has learned a lot about disability and a lot about diversity and tolerance and understanding."

BEING CONNECTED

One of the strongest themes that runs through these stories is the way interdependence and being connected to others is part of all stages of motherhood for women with disabilities. In Part One, Chris in her advice to prospective disabled mothers cautioned them to plan carefully for the help they will need for physical tasks when they return from the hospital with their child. Talia, who was overwhelmed at first with her newborn, says she was rescued by a doula [trained assistant for new mothers]. Later she found that other disabled

97

mothers helped her to feel confident about herself as a mother. She says, "I just might not do [the tasks of mothering] like anyone else, but it is my way. And it is making us a closer family."

The mothers in Part Two describe arrangements of shared care giving as children become more mobile and more physically demanding. The need to both give and receive care is illustrated by Kate's story as a single mother, balancing her daughter's needs with her own need for care. She says, "I think the biggest struggle for us with my disability has been that we needed people [personal care assistants] in the house." Cindy, Lorrie, and Tammy tell of shared parenting as couples and some of the tensions and satisfactions of working together to build a family. Whether the women are sharing with able-bodied partners or disabled partners, they express a sense of the importance of their own role. Cindy insists, "I am the mother" and Lorrie, who credits the help she gets from her able-bodied husband, says, "He's still not the mom."

Phouvieng, who said "I did not expect to raise my daughters by myself," did not have the connections that most of the mothers had. Separated from her common law husband, she was not supported by her Laotian community or by any social services. However, she speaks of the bond she has with her daughters: "I mean it is just amazing." Recently she has joined a church and has found some support and community there.

The stories in Part Three show how mothers with disabilities are motivated to move out of their own private sphere to connect to a larger world, and how they aspire to take their children with them. When their children go to school and experience the public scrutiny of their mothers or parents, these women help their children learn about how society defines "the norm," which includes having able-bodied parents. Lily describes an incident at her daughter's school. She heard a woman instruct her little girl not to stare at Lily because "she is not normal." Lily was quick to respond to her: "Who are you to say what is normal in society? Describe normal to me… I'm normal, just as you."

Many of the women become role models as advocates for diversity and specifically for people with disabilities. Lily explains that her advocacy for the rights and appreciation of people with disabilities began when she became active in organizations in her daughter's school and then moved on to larger public forums. Ellen and Beatrice, who both have children with a disability, speak of doing double advocacy: advocating for themselves and for their children in their schools. In contrast, Patti, who is blind, tells of living in a special community for the blind with her husband, also visually impaired, and bringing up their children where a disability was the "norm."

Continuing the theme of connecting in Part Four, mothers describe how they create an environment for their teenagers and young adults that embodies cooperation and an appreciation for the needs of others. Dorothy, a single mother, describes working with her teenage son in a partnership that balances his concern with taking care of her with his need to be independent. Donna and Janice create expanded communities for their families by adopting other children from diverse backgrounds. Donna brings up her children in co-housing and merges a part of her professional life as a swimming coach with her family. Bernice, raised in the projects in Roxbury —a community that took care of each other—extended this community to her daughter.

These women's stories show their determination to overcome physical, emotional and psychological challenges. They want to pass that determination to prevail on to their children but they want them to help others to succeed as well. Donna told her students that there is no such word as "can't" but she also explains that they must help each other and take responsibility for fellow students.

These women reject the label of "victim" but they equally reject the label of "martyr" or saint. Most of them share the consciousness of the disability movement, which redefines the notion that a person with a disability is a marginal person to be pitied and perhaps admired for being brave. Rather, they argue a person's disability is largely a social construction. A disabled person is a contributing member of society if given the necessary support. These mothers demand changes in society that can enable them to realize their full potential of being mothers, which includes their differences.

The contribution these women make to the definition of the role of mothering is the sense of the importance, indeed the necessity, of connecting with others and the realization that we are all interdependent as mothers. This notion contrasts with the often isolated and self-centered "nuclear family" model where a mother's role is strictly focused on her own children and family's success. Despite experiences of marginalization in their own lives, these women embrace interconnection while reaching out to offer their creative skills of adaptability. They provide a compelling model of mothering.

Chapter Six

Public Policy and Mothers with Disabilities

Linda Long-Bellil

There has been substantial progress in social policy with regard to individuals with disabilities over the past forty years. However little of the activism and innovation that has brought these changes about has focused specifically on the needs and rights of mothers with disabilities. Rather, mothers with disabilities are left to avail themselves of broader social policies that affect people with disabilities and mothers as separate categories, but rarely address their needs as a discrete group. This chapter describes how these discrete areas of policy address, or conversely, ignore the interests of mothers with disabilities, with a focus on the mothers with physical disabilities that are the subject of this book, and how more unified policies targeted specifically to the needs of this group could more effectively provide support and empowerment for them and their families

OVERVIEW OF CURRENT POLICIES TARGETED TO PERSONS WITH DISABILITIES

The World Health Organization conceptualizes disability as a complex interaction between personal and environmental factors that ultimately affect the individual's ability to assume typical social roles and otherwise participate in society (World Health Organization, 2002). Disability policy is comprised of a patchwork of laws and policies that affect individuals with a wide range of abilities and limitations and impact them at the personal and environmental levels in ways that do not always appear to serve the same set of goals (Burkhauser and Daly, 2002). Some policies provide support for basic subsistence and health care. These policies include the provision of income supports through programs such as Social Security Disability Insurance and Supplemental Security Income (Burkhauser and Daly, 2002). The first of these programs provides income to individuals with disabilities who have worked and paid Social Security taxes. The latter provides income to individuals with disabilities with low incomes. Both programs essentially define disability as the inability to work. The SSDI program, but not the SSI program, provides an additional benefit for the minor children of beneficiaries and spouses caring for them.

These policies also include programs that provide health coverage, most notably Medicare and Medicaid. Medicare is a federally funded and administered program that provides medical coverage to individuals with disabilities who receive Social Security Disability Insurance. It does not provide health coverage to the minor children or spouses of individuals who become disabled. Medicaid provides medical coverage to adults and children with disabilities (and also pregnant women and mothers living with their children, who qualify under separate criteria). Mothers who qualify for Medicaid because they have disabilities do not automatically receive Medicaid for their children, but their children can be covered by Medicaid under other programs. Certain Medicaid services such as hospital services and physician services must be provided in every state, but states have discretion over whether they offer certain services, such as personal assistance services.

Other more recent policies are intended to prohibit discrimination against people with disabilities, thereby supporting their participation in the community and assumption of typical social roles such as that of worker. The most prominent of these laws is the American with Disabilities Act (ADA) of 1990. Similar to the Civil Rights Act of 1964, the ADAprohibits discrimination against individuals with disabilities by places of public accommodation and employers. It also prohibits discrimination by state and municipal governments. Another law which supports community participation is the Rehabilitation Act, which provides for services to assist people with disabilities to become employed, to live independently in the community and similar programs. Section 504 of the Rehabilitation Act was essentially a precursor to the ADA and prohibits discrimination against individuals with disabilities by entities that receive federal funds.

OVERVIEW OF POLICIES REGARDING MOTHERS

Much of modern policy regarding mothers centers around policies that originated in the late 19th and early 20th centuries and were intended to assist single mothers and widows who were desperately poor and living with their children in squalid and unsafe conditions. The compassion that underlay some of these policies, particularly welfare policy, was mixed with a healthy dose of what at least one author has described as the "moralistic" and harsh judgments of the women that were the intended beneficiaries (Levy and Michel, 2002; Gordon, 1994). Much of welfare policy was crafted to encourage "proper" behavior on behalf of the recipients of the public's largesse. Initially, support was provided to mothers with the intent to enable them to stay at home and raise their children in accordance with the social norms of the day. Over time, this perspective metamorphosed into an expectation that mothers would work or take affirmative steps to enable them to return to work and ultimately lose their "dependence" on public benefits (Gordon, 1994).

This latter perspective informed the development of child care policies and programs in the United States. Unlike like some Western democracies, the U.S. does not take a universalist approach to publicly subsidized child care for all, but rather targets public financing for child care to low-income families, particularly those receiving welfare, with the intent of enabling parents to work (Mahon, 2002; Levy and Michel, 2002). Even within the limited scope of its reach, subsidized child care is chronically underfunded (Levy and Michel, 2002).

One of the most successful efforts to improve the wellbeing of women and children has been Title V of the Social Security Act and related programs administered through the Maternal and Child Health Bureau. Title V is "the only federal legislation that focuses solely on improving the health of mothers and children" (Health Resources and Services Administration, undated, p. 5). The majority of Title V funds are administered through its Maternal and Child Health Block Grant program, which is a federal-state partnership designed to support core public health functions and provide a broad array of critical services to pregnant women, mothers and children ranging from the Bright Futures for Women's Health and Wellness program, which encourages women's utilization of preventive health services, to the Women, Infants and Children (WIC) program, one of Title V's better known programs. An important Title V initiative is the Children with Special Health Care Needs program which supports the development and implementation of health care and related programs for children, many of which could be considered children with disabilities or at risk of disabilities. Title V programs such as these and other programs administered or funded by the Maternal and Child Health Bureau have made dramatic improvements in the survival and wellbeing of generations of mothers and children (Health Resources and Services Administration, undated).

Nevertheless, this program represents a good example of the bifurcation of programs serving mothers and programs serving individuals with disabilities. Although mothers with disabilities may by happenstance be among the women it serves, it does not target any programs specifically to them and the primary way that it serves individuals with disabilities is through its programs serving children with special health care needs (Health Resources and Services Administration, undated). In this respect, it misses an opportunity to fill critical gaps in the supports available to mothers with disabilities and their children. This dichotomy is typical of federal and state policies that, with improved coordination, could better support the needs of mothers with disabilities and their families. The remainder of this chapter will explore this issue, using the framework guiding the previous chapters as an organizing structure.

THE DECISION TO HAVE A CHILD AND THE GENETIC QUESTION

Advances in technology combined with the constitutionally-protected right to decide whether to bring a pregnancy to term give women with disabilities, and all women, an unprecedented amount of information and choice regarding bearing a child, including the decision to bear a child that may have a disability. The meaning and implications of the decisions women make with this newfound information and freedom are hotly debated (Parens and Asch, 2000). Some in the disability community assert that the use of prenatal diagnosis, in and of itself, devalues the lives of people with disabilities, while others assert that it merely enables people to make informed choices (Parens and Asch, 2000). Even those who take the latter view acknowledge that the information available to parents is often limited and biased, raising the question of the whether the choices parents make are informed in the truest sense.

Although there were a handful of unintended pregnancies among the women in this study, none of the women interviewed described feeling an obligation to bring their children to term, but rather chose quite affirmatively to do so. The women with genetic conditions in particular spoke of evaluating the choice to have a child in light of the value they placed on their own lives and believing that they could enable a child with the same disability to have a good life. In a sense, they had an advantage over the majority of mothers who have little or no experience with disability because their decision making was based upon firsthand knowledge about living with a disability, rather than assumptions that may have little or no basis in the actual lived experience of persons with disabilities (Parens and Asch, 2000). Although the public policies promoting choice and the development of technology giving women information about the possibility of disability meant that these women were presented with choices that many would find painful, tor the women in this study, the freedom to choose and to have information about their developing fetuses seemed empowering.

PREGNANCY, BIRTH AND POST PARTUM EXPERIENCE

Although modern medicine provides women with volumes of information about the characteristics of the children they are carrying, it seemed that medical providers often provided women in this study with little information about what to expect during pregnancy and childbirth. Many of the women in the study described their physicians' lack of knowledge and preparation regarding the impact of their disabilities on pregnancy and childbirth and were at times in the position of having to educate their physicians and other medical providers.

Provider Knowledge and Preparation

There is increasing recognition of this knowledge gap, not only with respect to the impact of disability on obstetrics/gynecology, but in all areas of medical care. In her 2006 article in the New England Journal of Medicine, Iezzoni (2006) notes that "although physicians learn volumes about treating underlying causes, many receive little training in addressing resultant disability" (p. 977). In 2005, the Surgeon General addressed this problem, issuing his *Call to Action to Improve the Health and Wellness of Persons with Disabilities*, which noted that "individuals with disabilities often encounter professionals unprepared to identify and treat their primary and secondary conditions and any other health and wellness concerns" (p.11). More recently, in 2009, the National Council on Disability issued its report *The Current State of Health Care for People with Disabilities*. One of its key findings was that "the absence of professional training on disability competency issues for health care practitioners is one of the most significant barriers that prevent people with disabilities from receiving appropriate and effective health care" (p. 1).

At the medical school level, there have been isolated efforts by faculty across the country, including some who are themselves individuals with disabilities or family members of individuals with disabilities. One example includes the standardized patient program at Tufts University School of Medicine where individuals with disabilities play the role of patient in a simulated medical interview conducted by third and fourth year medical students as part of the Family Medicine Clerkship (Minihan, 2004). Several such programs exist across the country as do programs that use other teaching modalities. For example at the University of South Florida, there is a clerkship for third year medical students that covers disability using methods ranging from home visits and service learning opportunities to lectures (Iezzoni, 2006). In general, these isolated efforts are the only exposure to disability that medical students receive during medical school. One exception is the School of Medicine of the University at Buffalo which recently instituted an integrated four year curriculum on physical disability (Symons, McGuigal and Akl, 2009).

Recently, a handful of organized efforts have arisen to address the provider training issue. The National Curricular Initiative in Developmental Medicine (NCIDM) is an effort by several organizations to design a model curriculum for residency education. The Alliance for Disability in Health Care Education is developing competencies for education of medical, nursing and certain other health professions students. The NCIDM effort is being funded by the Walmart Foundation. Funding for such efforts has otherwise generally been scarce, but in 2010, the Patient Protection and Affordable Care Act authorized funding to create model health professions curricula on disability. Unfortunately, at the time of this writing, funding had not yet been appropriated for this initiative.

In addition to these efforts, which are targeted largely to medical school students and residents, an effort to provide disability-related information to physicians at all levels, including practicing physicians, was recently undertaken by the American College of Obstetricians and Gynecologists, which has created a comprehensive web-based resource list for health care providers including some training modules. This resource list also includes information for women with disabilities on issues related to reproductive health, childbirth and childrearing. These developments represent meaningful progress on this issue, but there remains much work to be done.

In addition to physician organizations such as ACOG, maternal and child health programs at local departments of public health can also assist in raising the awareness of providers of the specific needs of mothers with disabilities during pregnancy, through childbirth and into the postpartum period. Maternal and children health programs frequently disseminate information about prenatal care and early childhood and could include information regarding women with disabilities in these programs (Downs, 2010).

There are nascent efforts to educate other health professionals of critical importance to individuals with disabilities, such as nurses and occupational therapists. Villanova University School of Nursing is instituting a standardized patient program to educate nurse practitioner students about working with patients with disabilities (Smeltzer, 2009). In addition, efforts have arisen to educate occupational therapy students and practitioners about evaluating the needs of and assisting parents with disabilities to perform their parenting tasks (National Resource Center for Parents with Disabilities, 2010).

RAISING A CHILD: CAREGIVING AND MOTHERS WITH DISABILITIES

The mothers in this study had to work around both the perception that they were unable to care for their children and actual barriers to doing so. Several of the women interviewed described how they improvised various ways of managing the physical care of their children. Although many of the women managed quite well on their own and might balk at the idea of assistance, others noted that some information and guidance might be helpful and seemed to welcome the idea that their ingenuity could potentially be enhanced by professional assessment and advice regarding assistive technology, adaptive equipment or other services that could facilitate their caretaking.

Assistive Technology and Services

Greater access to assistive technology, also described sometimes as "adaptive equipment," is one mechanism that the mothers in this study mentioned as potentially helpful. Current law provides limited support for efforts to make assistive technology available to persons with disabilities. Assistive technology (AT) means "any item, piece of equipment, or product system, whether acquired commercially off the shelf, modified, or customized that is used to increase, maintain, or improve the functional capabilities of individuals with disabilities" (Technology-Related Assistance for Individuals with Disabilities Act, 1988). This language originates from the Technology-Related Assistance for Individuals with Disabilities Act (TECH Act), which funds state programs whose mission is to coordinate the provision of assistive technology to individuals with disabilities. Unfortunately, TECH Act programs do not directly pay for assistive technology. They work with state agencies and other entities to coordinate payment policy for AT and conduct outreach and other activities to ensure that assistive technology makes its way into the hands of those individuals with disabilities who need it and that individuals and professionals receive the training necessary to facilitate its appropriate use (Field and Jette, 2007).

Some have noted that although assistive technology is covered under Medicare, Medicaid and some private insurers, this coverage does not necessarily extend to equipment needed to care for children. Insurers, including Medicaid and Medicare have historically only paid for equipment and services that can be justified as "medically necessary" (Rhoades and Seller, 2003).

The definition of medical necessity frequently tends to be interpreted to include only those services that directly address physical and mental functioning, but not those needed primarily to enable individuals to fulfill typical social roles such as parenting and working. Narrow definitions of medical necessity by private insurers and in federal and state programs frequently permit reimbursement only for AT that can be justified on these more traditional, medically based grounds (Rhoads and Seller, 2000; Field and Jette, 2007).

A similar problem arises with regard to assistive technology services, which encompass evaluation, training and other services related to the use of a piece of assistive technology (29 U.S.C. Sec 2202(2)). Again, definitions of medical necessity may limit access when the stated need is parenting (Idaho Assistive Technology Project, Undated; Field and Jette, 2007).

One of the few ways in which the federal government has made a conscious and affirmative effort to target the needs of parents with disabilities, is through the auspices of the National Institute on Disability and Rehabilitation Research which as of 2008 began to provide funding to the National Center for Parents with Disabilities and Their Families, a project of "Through the Looking Glass" (TLG), a community-based non-profit that grew out of the independent living movement and which provides information on assistive technology and services and other services to parents with disabilities. Among the resources TLG has developed is a baby care assessment tool that can be used by occupational therapists to determine ways in which a mother could be assisted through the use of adaptive devices. It has developed an accompanying curriculum for use by occupational therapists and schools of occupational therapy. In addition, it has a book that illustrates several types of assistive devices that can be constructed to help with child care (National Center for Parents with Disabilities and Their Families, 2010). The National Center also provides legal consultation services to address the needs of parents with disabilities who find themselves in the midst of a child custody battle with either the state or another parent.

Through the Looking Glass provides important services to parents with disabilities. The ability of parents to make the best use of these services would certainly be enhanced if funding were available. Changes to the law that would broaden the definition of medical necessity to include services that facilitate one's fulfillment of typical social roles such as parenting would be an important step forward in ensuring that parents with disabilities can make the most of assistive technologies available to them.

Personal Assistance Services

Another way in which narrow definitions of medical necessity constrain the supports potentially available to mothers with disabilities is through their application to personal assistance services (PAS). Under current Medicaid law, medically necessary personal assistance services, also known as Personal Care Assistance (PCA) do not generally encompass activities related to parenting. Rather they focus on "activities of daily living" such as eating, bathing, toileting and on "instrumental activities of daily living" which encompass services such as cleaning, grocery shopping and activities necessary to maintain the individual's ability to survive in the community. The use of such services to assume typical social roles and facilitate participation in the community beyond simply living there rather than in an institution has been a topic of some controversy. For example, the use of personal assistance services to facilitate participation in employment has been an ongoing subject of debate (Ellison and Glazier, et al., 2010).

Changing policies with regard to personal assistance to provide in-home care for children of parents with disabilities could be challenging in a policy environment where even funding for center-based child care is in short supply. The province of Ontario, Canada, has responded to this challenge by creating a program of "Nurturing Assistance" whereby personal assistance users are permitted to use a certain number of hours of personal assistance that have been approved to meet their personal needs for child care. This results not in the approval of additional hours in order to meet their child care needs, but in a reallocation of their existing hours (Prillitensky, 2004). In this way, the Nurturing Assistance program balances the needs of mothers with disabilities with concerns regarding financing and equity among those in need of child care.

Maternal and Child Health and Independent Living Services

Although funding constraints might make it challenging, a positive change to policy would be to enable maternal and child health programs to serve as a funding source for assistive technology and services when efforts to obtain it through other means have been unsuccessful. In addition to providing equipment, the evaluation, assessment and training aspects of using assistive technology could perhaps be integrated into existing home visiting programs and other maternal and child health services. TECH Act programs could help to define the roles of various state agencies in providing these services and assist in determining when and how maternal and child health agencies can play an appropriate role.

One of the mothers mentioned that she felt very isolated upon bringing her child home and that she would have appreciated the opportunity to talk with other mothers with disabilities. An appropriate and relatively inexpensive maternal and child health service could create such programs. These could be provided by the maternal and child health agencies themselves or they could provide an opportunity for cross-agency collaboration between departments of public health and agencies such as independent living centers. The latter are community-based organizations that provide peer counseling, of which support groups could be seen as an example, as a core service. Independent living centers could also provide programs where experienced mothers with disabilities could mentor newer mothers. Either approach would assist in reducing the isolation that some mothers with disabilities experience.

Involvement with Child Welfare Services

Although only one mother in the study was actually involved with child welfare services, and that was with regard to an older child where the concern was that the child was providing care to the mother, several of the mothers mentioned their concern that at some point they might come to the attention of child welfare services because of the perception that they were unable to care for their children. They described how, at times, this concern motivated them to ensure that the public face of their families was as close to "normal" as possible. This concern was not unfounded. Historically, mothers with disabilities have indeed had more to fear from the child welfare system. In a comprehensive review of state child welfare statutes, Lightfoot and LaLiberte (2006) noted that eight states specifically listed physical disability alone, without any other apparent factors, as grounds for removal of a child. The number of state statutes authorizing removal was even higher among mothers with psychiatric and intellectual disabilities (Lightfoot and LaLiberte, 2006).

Even if there is no specific language regarding physical disability in any given state statute, mothers with disabilities may face substantial hurdles in child custody proceedings. Child protective services workers "may have set beliefs about people with various disabilities or lack expertise in working with them" (Kay, 2009). In addition, although families are entitled to family preservation and reunification services, the degree to which such services must be modified to meet any disability-related needs that the family may have is unclear.

The Americans with Disabilities Act (ADA) prohibits discrimination against persons with disabilities. Title II of the ADA applies to state governments and requires that they ensure that "no qualified individual with a disability shall, by reason of such disability, be excluded from participation in or be denied the benefits of the services, programs, or activities of a public entity, or be subjected to discrimination by any such entity" (Americans with Disabilities Act, 1990). However, the courts are divided on the degree to which the ADA applies to family preservation and reunification services and whether it requires additional services not ordinarily provided or merely modifications to existing services (Kay, 2009; Callow, 2009). The unsettled state of the law leaves parents with disabilities in a precarious position should they come to the attention of state child welfare agencies. Regulations making it clear how the ADA applies to family preservation and reunification services would be an important step forward in ensuring that families in which the parents have disabilities have the best chance of remaining intact.

How much help should children give their disabled mother or parent?

Only a handful of the women interviewed were the mothers of pre-teens or teenagers. Some had resolved the issue of the child's role in participating in household chores and providing assistance to the parent in a manner that appeared acceptable to all concerned, while others struggled with this issue.

Research and policy in the United States on the phenomenon of children caring for their adult parents with disabilities is in its nascency (National Alliance for Caregiving, 2005). The number of children caring for parents or other adults in the household, e.g. grandparents, has been estimated at 1.3 to 1.4 million children under the age of 18 nationwide (National Alliance for Caregiving, 2005). In a 1997 survey funded by NIDRR and using a convenience sample of parents with disabilities, 44% of respondents reported receiving assistance in meeting personal needs from their children (Toms Barker and Maralini, 1997). The survey did not contain information about the nature or degree of assistance received.

This issue came to the attention of policymakers in other western countries such as the United Kingdom and Australia in the 1990s and these nations have made significant strides in addressing the needs of those whom they describe as "young carers" and their parents in ways that lend themselves to preserving family unity (National Alliance for Caregiving, 2005). These nations have devised a variety of strategies for addressing the issue such as support groups, Internet chat groups, writing, dramatic and artistic projects and activities for the whole family. The National Alliance for Caregiving, a non-profit coalition of national organizations focusing on issues of family caregiving, has noted that the United States would be well advised to implement such strategies in order to enhance the physical and psychological wellbeing of young people who provide care to their parents and, indeed, the entire family (National Alliance for Caregiving, 2005).

CONCLUSION

Mothers with disabilities are a resourceful group and manage to raise their families using their own ingenuity and, when necessary, by cobbling together supports from a variety of sources. A more organized, unified approach to public policy that affirmatively supports their efforts could play a valuable role in ensuring that existing resources from the disability, maternal and child health and related service systems are made more readily available to mothers with disabilities and that physicians and other key medical providers are better prepared to meet their needs. Just as public policy has evolved in the direction of encouraging individuals with disabilities to participate in employment and embrace the role of worker, so it should also move in the direction of supporting the equally valuable social role of mother and en-

hance the ability of women with disabilities to participate in this most funda-
mental and rewarding of human experiences.

Resources

Through the Looking Glass (The National Center for Parents with Disabilities and Their Families). Available at: http://www.lookingglass.org/ .
Through the Looking Glass has been a pioneer in the field of research,
services and supports for parents with disabilities. Services include assistive
technology/adaptive equipment, peer support, legal consultation for parents
with disabilities and college scholarships for their children. 2198 Sixth
Street, Suite 100, Berkeley, CA 94710-2204. Phone: 1-800-644-2666 (v),
TTY: 1-800-804-1616

The American College of Obstetricians and Gynecologists Women with
Disabilities Home Page. Available at http://www.acog.org/About_ACOG/
ACOG_Departments/Women_with_Disabilities . This web page offers comprehensive resources for clinicians and women with disabilities in the area of
obstetrics/gynecology and reproductive health.

Center for Research on Women with Disabilities (CROWD) Available at:
http://www.bcm.edu/crowd/index.cfm?PMID=1515 . This research center at
the Baylor College of Medicine: Center focuses on health and wellness,
sexuality, independent living and a variety of issues. Department of Physical
Medicine and Rehabilitation, Baylor Medical College, 3440 Richmond, Suite
B, Houston TX 77064, Phone: (713) 960-0505 (V), Director: Margaret Nosek, PhD.

Association of Assistive Technology Act Programs. Available at: http://
www.ataporg.org/index.html *Provides information about assistive technology programs.*

Disability in Pregnancy and Childbirth (2007) by Stella Frances McKay-
Moffat BA(Hons) MPhil FPCert CertEd RN RM ADM, Editor. Churchill
Livingstone. This book by a British midwife advises health care profession-
als on the needs of women with disabilities during pregnancy and childbirth.

The Disabled Woman's Guide to Pregnancy and Birth (2006) by Judith
Rogers. Written by a mother with a disability who holds the titles of Pregnancy and Parenting Specialist and Parenting Equipment Specialist at Through
the Looking Glass. Demos Medical Publishing. 368 Park Avenue South,
Suite 201, New York, New York. 10016

A Providers Guide for the Care of Women with Physical Disabilities and Chronic Conditions (2005) by Suzanne C. Smeltzer, SC and Nancy C. Harts-Shopko. Developed by the North Carolina Office on Disability and Health in collaboration with Villanova University College of Nursing. This publication provides guidance to providers on a variety of issues related to health care for women with disabilities, including pregnancy and childbirth. Available at http://projects.fpg.unc.edu/~ncodh/pdfs/providersguide.pdf.

Parenting: Tips from Parents (Who Happen to Have a Disability) on Raising Children (1989) by Betty Garee. A collection of articles and information on having and raising children, written by parents with disabilities. Accent Books/Cheever Publishing. PO Box 700, Bloomington, IL 61702. Phone (309)378-2961.

Works Cited

INTRODUCTION

Campbell, F. K. (2008). Refusing able(ness): A preliminary conversation about ableism. *A Journal of Media and Culture*, 11, (2), 3-4. Retrieved 1/16/09 from http://journal.media-culture.org.au/index.php/mcjournal/article/viewArticle/46.

Collins, C. (1999). Reproductive technologies for women with physical disabilities. *Sexuality and Disability*, 17, (4), 299-307.

Davis, L. (2000). Bodies of difference: Politics, disability and representation. In S. Snyder, B. Bruggemann, & R. Garland-Thomson, R. (Eds.). *Disability studies: Enabling the humanities* (pp.100-109). New York: The Modern Language Assoc. of America.

Gill, C. J. (2002). The last sisters: Health issues of women with disabilities. *DAWN ONTARIO: Disabled Women's Network*. Retrieved February 2002 from http://dawn.thot.netgill_pub/html.

Herndl, D. P, (2002). Reconstructing the posthuman feminist body twenty years after Audre Lorde's cancer journals. *Disability studies: Enabling the humanities* (pp.144-156). New York: The Modern Language Assoc. of America.

Hillyer, B. (1993). *Feminism and disability*. Norman: University of Oklahoma Press.

Madorsky, J.G. (February, 1995). Influence of disability on pregnancy and motherhood. *The Western Journal of Medicine*, 162, (2), 153 (2).

Mullin, A. (2005) *Reconceiving pregnancy and childcare ethics, experience and reproductive labor*. Cambridge: Cambridge University Press.

Olsen, R. & Clarke, H. (2003). *Parenting and disability: Disabled parents' experience of raising children*. Bristol: The Policy Press.

Prilleltensky, O. (Spring, 2003.) A ramp to motherhood: The experience of mothers with physical disabilities. *Sexuality and Disability*, 21, (1), 212-23.

Richman, S. (2005). When your ob/gyn patient happens to be disabled. *Contemporary OB/GYN*. Retrieved February 28, 2005 from http://obgyn.adv100 .com/obgyn/content/printContentPopup.jsp?id=145656.

Ruddick, Sara. (1995). *Maternal thinking: Toward a politics of peace*. Boston: Beacon Press.

Garland-Thomson, R. (1997). *Extraordinary bodies: Figuring physical disability in American culture and literature*. New York: Columbia University Press.

Wendell, S. (1997). Toward a feminist theory of disability. In L.J. Davis (Ed,) *The Disability Studies Reader* (pp. 260-279). New York: Routledge.

CHAPTER 1

Asch, A. & Fine, M. (1997). Nurturance, sexuality and women with disabilities. In L. J. Davis (Ed.). *The disability studies reader* (p.24). New York: Routledge.

Center for Research on Women with Disabilities (CROWD) (2009). *Health care-medical professionals' knowledge about the health of women with disabilities.* Baylor College of Medicine. Retrieved 5/17/09 from http://www.bcm.edu/crowd//pmid=143#top.

Finger, A. (1990). *Past due: A story of disability, pregnancy and birth.* Seattle: The Seal Press.

Hubbard, Ruth (1997). Abortion and disability. In L.J. Davis (Ed.) *The disability studies reader* (p. 199). New York: Routledge.

Jacobsen, D. Sherer (1999). *The question of David: A disabled mother's journey through adoption, family and life* (pp.182-183). Berkeley: Creative Arts Book Company.

Kelleher, C, M. (2003). *Postpartum matters: women's experiences of medical surveillance, time and support after birth.* Unpublished doctoral dissertation, Brandeis University.

Kent, D. (Spring, 2002). Beyond expectations: Being blind and becoming a mother. *Sexuality and Disability*, 20 (1). 81-88.

Litwinowiz, J. (1999). In my mind's eye: Pre-pregnancy and becoming a parent. In M. Wates, & R.Jade (Eds.). *Bigger than the sky: Disabled women on parenting* (pp. 29-34). London: The Women's Press.

Norsigian, J. & Potter, J. (June 12, 2009). A singular solution for healthcare. *The Boston Globe.* p. A11.

Prilleltensky O. (Spring, 2003). A ramp to motherhood: The experiences of mothers with physical disabilities. *Sexuality and Disability* 27 (1) 21-39.

Rogers, Judith(2006), *The disabled woman's guide to pregnancy and birth.* New York: Demos Health.

CHAPTER 2

Davis, Barbara Hillyer (1984). Women, disability and feminism: Notes toward a new theory. *Frontiers: A Journal of Women Studies* 8 (1), 1.

Grue, L. & Laerum, K. T. (2002). Doing motherhood: some experiences of mothers with physical disabilities. *Disability and Society*, 17(6), 671-68.

Mairs, N. (1995). *Waist high in the world: A life among the disabled.* Boston: Beacon Press.

Mullin, A. (2005). *Reconceiving pregnancy and childcare: Ethics, experience and reproductive labor.* Cambridge: Cambridge University Press.

Watson, N., McKie, L., Hughes, B., Hopkins, D., & Gregory, S. (2001). (Inter)Dependence needs and care: The potential for disability and feminist theorists to develop an emancipatory model. *Sociology*, 38(2). Sage Publications.

Wendell, Susan (1997). Toward a feminist theory of disability. In Davis, L.J. (Ed.), *The disability studies reader.* New York: Routledge.

CHAPTER 3

Collins, P. Hill. (1991). *Black feminist thought: Knowledge, consciousness and the politics of empowerment.* New York: Routledge.

Johnson, Harriet McBryde. (2003, February 16). Unspeakable conversations or How I spent one day as a token cripple at Princeton University. *The New York Times Magazine.* 50-58.

Najarian, C. (2006), *Between worlds: Deaf women, work and intersection of gender and ability.* New York: Routledge.

Ruddick Sara R. (1995). *Maternal thinking: Toward a politics of peace.* Boston: Beacon Press.

Garland-Thomson, R. (2009) *Staring: How we look.* New York: Oxford University Press.

Wates, M, (1999). Are you sure you can cope? In M. Wates, & J. Rowen, (Eds.), *Bigger than the sky: Disabled women on parenting.* London: The Women's Press.

CHAPTER 4

Black, K. (1996). *In the shadow of polio: A personal and social history.* New York: Addison Wesley Publishing Company.

Davis, L.J. (2000). *My sense of silence: Memoirs of a childhood with deafness.* Chicago: University of Illinois Press.

Mullin, A. (2005). *Reconceiving pregnancy and childcare: Ethics, experience and reproductive labor.* Cambridge: Cambridge University Press.

Newman, T. (2002) Young carers and disabled parents: Time for a change of direction? *Disability and Society* (17), 613-625.

Twardowski, B. and J. (2005) Raising teens: Is it different for parents with disabilities? *Quest* (12)1.

CHAPTER 6

Americans with Disabilities Act, 42 U.S.C. § 12132, 1990.

Callow, E. (2009) *Representing parents with disabilities in the child welfare system.* ABA Center on Children and the Law: First National Parents' Attorneys Conference (May 13, 2009). Washington, D.C.

Diaz, N., Siskowski, E.C., and Connors, E.L. (2007) Latino young caregivers in the United States: Who are they and what are the academic implications of this role? *Child Youth Care Forum.* 36, 131–140.

Ellison M. L, Glazier R. E, O'Connell E, Norton G, Himmelstein J. Design features for employment-supportive personal assistance services in Medicaid programs. *Journal of Disability Policy Studies*, in press. 2010.

Field, M. J. and Jette, A. M. (Eds.). (2007) *The future of disability in America.* Washington, D.C.: Institute of Medicine.

Gordon, L. (2004) *Pitied but not entitled: Single mothers and the history of welfare.* New York: The Free Press.

Levy, D.U. and Michel, S. (2002) Child care and welfare reform in the United States. In S. Michel, & R. Mahon (Eds.). *Child care at the crossroads: Gender and welfare state restructuring.* (pp. 239-263). New York: Routledge.

Mahon, R. (2002) Introduction: Gender and Welfare State Restructuring. In Michel, S. and Mahon, R. *Child care at the crossroads: Gender and welfare state restructuring* (pp. 1-27). New York: Routledge.

Parens, E. and Asch, A. (2000) *Prenatal diagnosis and disability rights.* Washington, DC: Georgetown University Press.

Rhoads, L. & Seller, R.J. (2003). *Assistive technology for parents with disabilities: A handbook for parents, families, and caregivers.* Moscow, Idaho. Idaho Assistive Technology Project. Center on Disabilities and Human Development. University of Idaho.

Symons, A.B., McGuigan, D. and Akl, E.A. (2000), A curriculum to teach medical students to care for people with disabilities: Development and initial implementation. *BMC Medical Education.* Retrieved October 30, 2010 from http://www.ncbi.nlm.nih.gov/pmc/articles/PMC2809044/.

National Alliance for Caregiving (NAC) & The United Hospital Fund (UHF) (2005). *Young caregivers in the U.S.: Findings from a national survey.* Retrieved 11/14/06 from http://www.caregiving.org/data/youngcaregivers.pdf.

Technology-Related Assistance for Individuals with Disabilities Act, 29 U.S.C. § 2202(2), 1988.

The National Center for Parents with Disabilities and Their Families. (2010) *Services for Parents with Disabilities: Adaptive Equipment.* Retrieved 11/30/10 from http://www.lookingglass.org/services/local-services/services-for-parents-with-disabilities.

Toms Barker, L. and Maralini, V. (1997) *Challenges and strategies of disabled parents: Findings from a national survey of parents with disabilities.* Oakland, California: Berkeley Planning Associates.

World Health Organization. (2002) *Towards a common language for functioning: Disability and health.* Geneva, Switzerland: ICF World Health Organization.

Selected Bibliography

A journey to motherhood. *Parents with Disabilities Online*, Retrieved 4/6/05, from http://www.disabledparents.net/journeytomotherhood.html.

Asch, A. & Fine, M. (1997). Nurturance, sexuality and women with disabilities; the example of women and literature. In Lennard J. Davis (Ed.), *The disability studies reader* (pp. 241-260). New York: Routledge.

Black, K. (1996). *In the shadow of polio: A personal and social history*. New York: Addison Wesley Publishers.

Campbell, F. K. (2008). Refusing able(ness): A preliminary conversation about ableism. *A Journal of Media and Culture.* 11(3), 3-4.

Center for Research on Women with Disabilities (1999). *Pregnancy: National study of women with physical disabilities.* Retrieved June 30, 2004, from http://www.bcm.tmc.edu/crowd/national_study/PREGNANC.htm.

Center for Research on Women with Disabilities (CROWD). (2009). *Health care-medical professionals' knowledge about the health of women with disabilities.* Baylor College of Medicine, Houston, Texas. Retrieved 5/17/09 from http://www.bcm.edu/crowd//pmid=143#top.

Collins, C. (1999). Reproductive technologies for women with physical disabilities. *Sexuality and Disability,* 17(4), 299-307.

Collins, P. Hill (1991). *Black feminist thought: Knowledge, consciousness and the politics of empowerment.* New York: Routledge, Chapman and Hall.

Couser, G. T. (1997). *Recovering bodies: Illness, disability and life writing.* Madison: The University of Wisconsin Press.

Davis, L. J. (2000). Bodies of difference: Politics, disability and representation. In S L. Snyder, B. J. Brueggemann, R. G Thomson (Eds.), *Disability studies: Enabling the humanities* (100-109). New York: The Modern Language Association of America.

———. (1997). *The disability studies reader.* New York: Routledge.

———. (2000). *My sense of silence: Memoirs of a childhood with deafness.* Chicago: University of Illinois Press.

Finger, A. (1990). *Past due: A story of disability, pregnancy and birth.* Seattle: The Seal Press.

Finke, B. (2003). *Long time no see.* Chicago: University of Illinois Press.

Fleischer, D. Z. & Zames, F. (Eds.). (2001). *The disability rights movement: From charity to confrontation.* Philadelphia: Temple University Press.

Frank, A. W. (1995). *The wounded storyteller: Body, illness and ethics.* Chicago and London: University of Chicago Press.

Gill, C. J. (2002). The last sisters: Health issues of women with disabilities. *Disabled Women's Network.* Retrieved February, 2002, from http://dawn.thot.net/cgill_pub.html.

Grue, L. & Tajford Laerum, K. (2002). Doing motherhood: Some experiences of mothers with physical disabilities. *Disability and Society*, 17(6), 671-683.

Hanson, K. W. (1996, November). Sarah...the first two years (quadriplegic mother offers insights and advice). *Paraplegia News* 50 (11), pp. 76 (4). Retrieved 9/27/06, from http://find.galegroup.com//ips/printdoc.do?&prodId=IPS&usergroup.

Hathaway, K. B. (2000). *The little locksmith: A memoir*. New York: The Feminist Press: The City University of New York.

Herndl, D. P. (2002). Reconstructing the posthuman feminist body twenty years after Audre Lorde's cancer journals. *Disability studies: Enabling the humanities*, New York: The Modern Language Association of America, pp 144-156.

Hillyer, B. (1993). *Feminism and disability*. Norman: University of Oklahoma Press.

Hubbard, R. (1997). Abortion and disability. In Lennard J. Davis (Ed.), *The disability studies reader* (p. 199). New York: Routledge.

Iezzoni, L. (2006). Going beyond disease to address disability. *New England Journal of Medicine*, 355(10), 976-979.

———. (2003). *When walking fails: Mobility problems of adults with chronic conditions*. Berkeley: The University of California Press.

Jacobsen, D. S. (1997). *The question of David: A disabled mother's journey through adoption, family and life*. Berkeley: Creative Arts Book Company.

Jeremiah, E. (2006). Motherhood to mothering and beyond: Maternity in recent feminist thought, mothering and feminism. *Journal of the Association of Research on Mothering*, 8(1,2), 21-34.

Kay, J.B. (Fall, 2009). Representing parents with disabilities in child protection proceeding. *The Michigan Child Welfare Law Journal*, Vol XIII(1), 27-36.

Keith, L. (Ed.). (1996). *What happened to You?: Writing by disabled women*. London: The Women's Press.

Kelleher, C. M. (2003). *Postpartum matters: Women's experiences of medical surveillance, time and support after birth*. Unpublished doctoral dissertation, Brandeis University.

Kent, D. (2002). Beyond expectations: being blind and becoming a mother. *Sexuality and Disability*, 20 (1), pp. 81-88.

Killoran, C. (1994). Women with disabilities having children: It's our right too. *Sexuality and Disability*, 12(2), 121-126.

Kilson, M. & Ladd, F. (2009). *Is that your child?: Mothers talk about rearing biracial children*. Lanham, Md: Lexington Books.

Kleege, G. (2006). *Blind rage: Letters to Helen Keller*. Washington: Gallaudet Press.

Kocher, M. (1994). Mothers with disabilities. *Sexuality and Disability*, 12 (2).

Landsman, G.(2008). *Reconstructing motherhood and disability in the age of "perfect babies."* New York: Routledge.

Lewieccki-Wilson, C. and Cellio, J. (Eds.). (2011). *Disability and mothering: Liminal spaces of embodied knowledge*. Syracuse: Syracuse University Press.

Linton, S. (2006). *My body politic: A memoir*. Ann Arbor: The University of Michigan Press.

Lipson, J. G. & Rogers, J. (2000). Pregnancy, birth, and disability: Womens' health care experiences. *Health Care for Women International*, 21(1), 11-26.

Litwinowiz, J. (1999). In my mind's eye: Pre-pregnancy and becoming a parent, In M. Wates & R. Jade (Eds.) *Bigger than the sky: Disabled women on parenting*. London: The Women's Press.

Longmore, P. & Umansky, L. (Eds.). (2001). *The new disability history: American perspectives*. New York: New York University Press.

Madorsky, J. G. (1995). Influence of disability on pregnancy and motherhood. *The Western Journal of Medicine*, 162(2), 153(2).

Mairs, N. (1987). *Plaintext: Deciphering a woman's life*. New York: Perennial Press.

———. (1990). *Remembering the bone house: An erotics of place and time*. Boston: Beacon Press.

———. (1996). *Waist-high in the world: A life among the nondisabled*. Boston: Beacon Press.

Malacrida, C. (2007). Negotiating the dependency/nurturance tightrope: Dilemmas of motherhood and disability. *Canadian Review of Sociology and Anthropology, CRSA/RCSA 44.42007.*

Mason, M. G. (2004). *Working against odds: Stories of disabled women's work lives.* Boston: Northeastern University Press.

Michel, S. & Mahon, R. (2002). *Child care at the crossroads: Gender and welfare state restructuring.* New York: Routledge.

Minihan P. M., et al (2004). Teaching about disability: Involving patients with disabilities as medical educators. *Disability Studies Quarterly* 24(4). Retrieved from http://www.dsq-sds.org/article/view/883/1058.

Mitchell, D.T. & Snyder, S. (Eds.). (1997). *The body and physical difference: Discourses of disability.* Ann Arbor: University of Michigan Press.

Morris, J. (Ed.). (1992). *Alone together: Voices of single mothers.* London: The Women's Press.

Mullin, A. (2005). *Reconceiving pregnancy and childcare ethics, experience and reproductive labor.* Cambridge: Cambridge University Press.

Najarian, C. (2006). *Between worlds: Deaf women, work and intersection of gender and ability.* New York: Routledge.

Newman, T. (2002). Young carers and disabled parents: Time for a change of direction. *Disability and Society,* 17(6), 613-625.

Norsigian, J. & Potter, J. (June 15, 2009). A singular solution for healthcare. *The Boston Globe,* p. A 11.

Olkin, R. & Abrams, K. (2004). The parents with disabilities and their teens project: Summary of results. Through the Looking Glass, Berkeley, CA.

Olsen, R. & Clarke, H. (2003). *Parenting and disability: Disabled parents' experience of raising children.* Bristol: The Policy Press.

Pendergrass, S., Nosek, M.A., & Holcomb, J.D. (2001). Design and evaluation of an internet site to educate women with disabilities on reproductive health care. *Sexuality and Disability,* 19(1), 71-83.

Potok, A. (2002). *A matter of dignity: Changing the world of the disabled.* New York: Bantam Books.

Prilleltensky, O. (2003). A ramp to motherhood: The experience of mothers with physical disabilities. *Sexuality and Disability,* 21, 1.

———. (2004). *Motherhood and disability: Children and choices.* London: Palgrave, Macmillan.

———. (2004). My child is not my career: Mothers with physical disabilities and the well-being of children. *Disability and Society,* 19(3).

Read, J. (2000). *Disability, the family and society: Listening to the mothers.* Philadelphia: Open University Press.

Richman, S. (2005). When your ob/gyn patient happens to be disabled. *Contemporary OB/GYN.* Retrieved February 28, 2005, from http://obgyn.adv100. com/obgyn/content/print-ContentPopup.jsp?id=145656.

Rogers, J. (2006). *The disabled woman's guide to pregnancy and birth.* New York: Demos Health.

Ruddick, S. (1995). *Maternal thinking: Toward a politics of peace.* Boston: Beacon Press.

Russell, M. (1998). *Beyond ramps: Disability at the end of the social contract.* Monroe, Me: Common Courage Press.

Snyder, S. L. & Brueggemann, B.J., Garland-Thomson, R. (Eds.). (2002). *Disability studies: Enabling the humanities.* New York: Modern Language Association of America.

Swain, P. A. & Cameron, C. (2003). "Good enough parenting": Parental disability and child protection. *Disability and Society,* 18(2), 165-177.

Through the Looking Glass. (2004). *The parents with disabilities and their teens project.* Berkeley, CA. Retrieved 5/4/08 from http://lookingglass.org/publications/summaryofresults.php .

Thomas, C. (1997). The baby and the bath water: Disabled women and motherhood in social context. *Sociology of Health and Illness,* 19(5), 622-643.

Thomson, R. G. (2006). Ways of staring. *Journal of Visual Culture,* 5(2), 173-182.

———. (1997). *Extraordinary bodies: Figuring physical disability in American culture.* New York: Columbia University Press.

———. (2009). Staring: How we look. New York: Oxford University Press.

Twardowski, B. & Twardowski, J. (2005). Raising teens: Is it different for parents with disabilities. *Quest,* 12(1).

Van *Kraayenoord, C. (2002). The media's portrayal of mothers with disabilities (editorial). International Journal of Disability,* 49(3), 221-222.

Wates, M. (1999). Are you sure you can cope? In M. Wates & R. Jade (Eds.), *Bigger than the sky: Disabled women and parenting* (pp. 94-101). London: The Women's Press.

Watson, N., McKie, L., Hughes, B., Hopkins, D., & Gregory, S. (2001). "(Inter)dependence needs and care: The potential for disability and feminist theorists to develop an emancipatory model. *Sociology,* (Sage Publications), 38(2).

Wendell, S. (1997). Toward a feminist theory of disability. In Lennard J. Davis (Ed.), *The disability studies reader.* (pp. 260-279) New York: Routledge.

Wong, A. (2000). The work of disabled women seeking reproductive health care. *Sexuality and Disability,* 18(4), 301-306.